# Christology

# Christology

## Key Readings in Christian Thought

EDITED BY

**Jeff Astley**
**David Brown**
**and Ann Loades**

First published in the United States of America in 2009 by
Westminster John Knox Press, Louisville, Kentucky

Published in Great Britain in 2009

Society for Promoting Christian Knowledge
36 Causton Street
London SW1P 4ST

See acknowledgements, pp. 109–11, for additional permission information.

*British Library Cataloguing-in-Publication Data*
A catalogue record for this book is available from the British Library

ISBN 978–0–281–06184–6

1 3 5 7 9 10 8 6 4 2

Book design by Sharon Adams

Printed in Great Britain by Ashford Colour Press

Produced on paper from sustainable forests

# Contents

# Preface

Courses in theology and religious studies in seminaries, colleges, and universities are increasingly "topic-based" or "problem-based." But there is a lack of easy to comprehend and easily accessible primary source material to help in studying these subjects. This means that teachers and students often turn to secondary sources, which can often fail to capture the sharpness and vitality of original theological thinking as it is forged in the crucibles of religious life and debate.

This volume on Christology is designed to meet this need by providing a set of carefully selected readings from primary sources, accompanied by a brief introductory essay, topics for discussion or further study, a glossary, and suggestions for further reading. This means the materials can be used either comprehensively, to suvey the whole field of Christian thinking about Jesus Christ, or selectively, focusing on specific problems or issues in the field of Christology.

The editors wish to thank all who have assisted in this project by helping in the selection, referencing, and trial-testing of material; by copy-typing, editing, and indexing the text; or by securing permissions. Particular thanks go to Evelyn Jackson, Rob MacSwain, and Maxwell Wood.

## Notes on the Text

The passages are printed (except for omissions, indicated by ellipsis points) as they were published in the original texts, with the same spelling and punctuation. In most cases, however, notes within the readings have been omitted. In a number of places the editors have added their own explanatory comments. These are normally printed in italics and are often enclosed within square brackets.

# Introduction

## Reading the Readings

Through most of Christian history the first three Gospels were read in the light of John (especially passages such as 1:1–18 or 8:52–59, with its reference back to the divine theophany in Exod. 3:14). A very high Christology was therefore presupposed. However, with the rise of biblical criticism from the eighteenth century onward, Mark came increasingly to be seen as the earliest Gospel. Theologians now confronted a text that at times appeared to pull in opposing directions: contrast, for example, Mark 6:5 and 13:32 with 4:41.[1] They now agreed that, to varying degrees, the Gospels had been written from the perspective of where the story ended, and so in the light of Jesus' resurrection. For the more liberal strand of Christianity that now emerged, this entailed the abandonment of any strict claim to divinity in Christ: divinity was essentially a powerful metaphor for Jesus' role as the medium or cipher through whom God had acted, and as such was traceable back to the New Testament itself, which had been wrongly read in ontological terms (see Hooker in section 1.1). While some continue to utilize the traditional arguments (e.g., Feenstra in 1.1), many now respond by taking the experience of the early disciples as normative. They were led to worship Christ, however much this might be framed in linguistic categories that seem strange to us today (Hurtado and Chester, in 1.1).

In their contributions to this debate, liberals and conservatives alike can sometimes be equally dismissive of the discussions in the early church that led to the classic formulations of the official position: during the first general Council at Nicaea (325), which helped to give us the creed of that name

---

1. The key biblical texts are all available in section 1.1.

(1.2), and at the Fourth Council at Chalcedon (451), which produced the so-called Chalcedonian Definition, with its demand that Christ be treated as both fully divine and fully human (1.4). Exception is taken to the introduction of nonbiblical and abstract terminology such as *homoousios*, the assertion that Christ is "of the same substance" or "being" as the Father. Those subsequently labeled heretics (Arius, Apollinarius, and Nestorius, in 1.2 and 1.3) were, however, for the most part devout Christians trying their best to make sense of the biblical evidence, while the church in its turn can be seen not as attempting a complete explanation but rather as seeking to impose limits on certain legitimate insights that had been carried to an extreme (so Norris and Coakley in 1.4). Even so, for some (e.g., Cupitt in 1.4) the resultant definition seems as senseless as combining square and circle, no matter how many philosophical qualifications are introduced (McCabe and Wiles in 1.4). The question, therefore, remains pertinent as to how far exploration in fresh conceptual terms should be pursued, and where acceptance of mystery ought to take over.

Because there is no commonly agreed way of justifying belief in Christ's divinity, with some denying that Jesus ever even claimed to be the Messiah, there is a temptation to cut the Gordian knot and deny that faith is dependent on the details of history. What matters is what the Gospels preach, and thus faith in the possibility of new life through Christ as proclaimed. This is the approach adopted by Rudolf Bultmann and Paul Tillich (in 2.1). While it fits well with their existentialist philosophy, the most obvious objection is that it seems to make Christ a projection of human experience rather than the Lord of history (Harvey and Tanner in 2.1). So, perhaps not surprisingly, there has in recent years been a strong revival of interest in the quest for the historical Jesus (now in its third variant). N. T. Wright is perhaps the best-known example (2.2). However, the pivotal role of the resurrection in Christian belief inevitably forces the discussion beyond the purely historical and into questions of theological significance. Although debate continues about whether or not it matters that the tomb was empty, clearly of more moment is what significance is to be attached to the vindication of Jesus in the new life that he now enjoys. Küng, Barth, and Pannenberg (in 2.3) offer rather different answers, with Pannenberg most insistent that the resurrection is decisive in asserting and defining Christ's divinity.

An account like Pannenberg's raises in an acute form what precisely was the relation between divinity and humanity in Christ during his earthly life. Some contemporary theologians continue to try to make sense of the classical expression of that relationship in Athanasius (e.g., Jennings in

3.1). But although Chalcedon had demanded the existence of a human soul in Christ, the tradition that developed viewed such a soul as essentially always fully subordinated to the divine nature and, indeed, in some senses its mere instrument. So, for example, Aquinas asserts that the human nature is always in possession of a perfect knowledge through infusion of such awareness from the divine. This is a position that sits uneasily with Jesus' apparent admission of things he does not or cannot know, still more so with his unawareness of his own divinity (as many modern scholars would now claim). The result has increasingly been an appeal to *kenosis*, or the "self-emptying" of divinity. The notion is not new. It derives ultimately from Paul in Philippians 2 (quoted in 1.1) and was subsequently put to use by theologians as different as Athanasius (3.1) and Calvin (3.2). What is new is the supposition that the divine nature does not merely show restraint in the exercise of its powers but actually holds back some of them from the human nature (Balthasar in 3.2) or, more radically, that the divine nature in some sense actually becomes human (P. T. Forsyth and Davis and Evans in 3.2). For many, the latter is altogether one step too far in its modification of our understanding of divinity (Cyril in 3.2), partaking—it would seem—more of the mythological than of the inspirational (Cupitt in 3.2). The difficulty with the alternative, however, is that it seems to leave us with a looser relation between the two natures than the church had advocated historically and so might be seen as calling into question the idea of Christ as one single person, both human and divine.[2]

But why should all of this matter? For Barth and Moltmann (3.3) the incarnation is crucial because it conveys something of vital importance about both God and human nature that can be adequately conveyed in no other way. As Farrer and Machen (3.4) make clear, the virginal conception of Jesus is best fitted within such a claim: this origin for Jesus perfectly encapsulates the idea of Christ as pure divine gift, unmediated and unqualified. The fundamental issue remains whether certain things can be said and done only by a personal divine act and not representatively through another (see Pailin and Hebblethwaite for opposing views, in 3.4).

There is no material specifically on atonement in this volume, not because the issue is unimportant but partly because it needs to be set in the wider context of being only one among several key factors for supposing that an incarnation might occur. Integral to the atonement is the claim for

---

2. For a philosophically sophisticated attempt to answer that objection, but one too difficult to extract briefly, see T. V. Morris, *The Logic of God Incarnate* (Ithaca, NY: Cornell University Press, 1986).

Christ of universal significance. Such a possibility has come increasingly under attack in recent years. In the final section a number of such challenges are explored, beginning with liberation theology (4.1). Here the claim (in Boff, Segundo, and Sobrino) is that Christ fails to be relevant to all humanity, especially the poor and oppressed, unless a political dimension is seen as no less integral than the personal. Laudable though such concerns are, Pope Benedict XVI and Balthasar express the concern that a new form of exclusivism might emerge in its turn, one that prevents the church from transcending conflict in a way that addresses the needs of all indifferently. Feminists raise the question of how women can be adequately included by a savior who was, after all, male rather than female. Christian feminists highlight elements of patriarchy that require removal (Ruether and Johnson at 4.2). Sometimes (e.g., Coakley) they also suggest that Christ's behavior in its self-offering was effectively a critique of his own sex and its characteristic assertiveness. Color and race can also be an issue (Grant, Melanchthon, and Oduyoye in 4.3), as can adherence to another religion. Earlier approaches canvassed three options: exclusivism, with Christianity seen as the only way to God; inclusiveness, which identified Christianity as the supreme but not only way; and pluralism, where all or several were seen as equally legitimate. Nowadays there is concern to get beyond such simple categories into what might be described as a more listening mode that assumes Christ's continuing relevance to other faiths but no longer pretends dogmatically to know in advance precisely where learning might occur and where teaching—in short, Christ as a presence alongside all humanity (O'Collins and Williams in 4.4).

# Chapter One

# The Shape of the Debate

## 1.1 The Biblical Christ

*Mark 4:35–41*

[35]On that day, when evening had come, he said to them, "Let us go across to the other side." [36]And leaving the crowd behind, they took him with them in the boat, just as he was. Other boats were with him. [37]A great gale arose, and the waves beat into the boat, so that the boat was already being swamped. [38]But he was in the stern, asleep on the cushion; and they woke him up and said to him, "Teacher, do you not care that we are perishing?" [39]He woke up and rebuked the wind, and said to the sea, "Peace! Be still!" Then the wind ceased, and there was a dead calm. [40]He said to them, "Why are you afraid? Have you still no faith?" [41]And they were filled with great awe and said to one another, "Who then is this, that even the wind and the sea obey him?"

*Mark 6:1–6*

[1]He left that place and came to his hometown, and his disciples followed him. [2]On the sabbath he began to teach in the synagogue, and many who heard him were astounded. They said, "Where did this man get all this? What is this wisdom that has been given to him? What deeds of power are being done by his hands! [3]Is not this the carpenter, the son of Mary and brother of James and Joses and Judas and Simon, and are not his sisters here with us?" And they took offense at him. [4]Then Jesus said to them, "Prophets are not without honor, except in their hometown, and among their own kin, and in their own house." [5]And he could do no deed

of power there, except that he laid his hands on a few sick people and cured them. <sup>6</sup>And he was amazed at their unbelief.

### Mark 8:27–33

<sup>27</sup>Jesus went on with his disciples to the villages of Caesarea Philippi; and on the way he asked his disciples, "Who do people say that I am?" <sup>28</sup>And they answered him, "John the Baptist; and others, Elijah; and still others, one of the prophets." <sup>29</sup>He asked them, "But who do you say that I am?" Peter answered him, "You are the Messiah." <sup>30</sup>And he sternly ordered them not to tell anyone about him.

<sup>31</sup>Then he began to teach them that the Son of Man must undergo great suffering, and be rejected by the elders, the chief priests, and the scribes, and be killed, and after three days rise again. <sup>32</sup>He said all this quite openly. And Peter took him aside and began to rebuke him. <sup>33</sup>But turning and looking at his disciples, he rebuked Peter and said, "Get behind me, Satan! For you are setting your mind not on divine things but on human things."

### Mark 13:30–32

<sup>30</sup>"Truly I tell you, this generation will not pass away until all these things have taken place. <sup>31</sup>Heaven and earth will pass away, but my words will not pass away.

<sup>32</sup>"But about that day or hour no one knows, neither the angels in heaven, nor the Son, but only the Father."

### Mark 15:31–39

<sup>31</sup>In the same way the chief priests, along with the scribes, were also mocking him among themselves and saying, "He saved others; he cannot save himself. <sup>32</sup>Let the Messiah, the King of Israel, come down from the cross now, so that we may see and believe." Those who were crucified with him also taunted him.

<sup>33</sup>When it was noon, darkness came over the whole land until three in the afternoon. <sup>34</sup>At three o'clock Jesus cried out with a loud voice, "Eloi, Eloi, lema sabachthani?" which means, "My God, my God, why have you forsaken me?" <sup>35</sup>When some of the bystanders heard it, they said, "Listen, he is calling for Elijah." <sup>36</sup>And someone ran, filled a sponge with sour wine,

put it on a stick, and gave it to him to drink, saying, "Wait, let us see whether Elijah will come to take him down." [37]Then Jesus gave a loud cry and breathed his last. [38]And the curtain of the temple was torn in two, from top to bottom. [39]Now when the centurion, who stood facing him, saw that in this way he breathed his last, he said, "Truly this man was God's Son!"

### *Matthew 28:16–20*

[16]Now the eleven disciples went to Galilee, to the mountain to which Jesus had directed them. [17]When they saw him, they worshiped him; but some doubted. [18]And Jesus came and said to them, "All authority in heaven and on earth has been given to me. [19]Go therefore and make disciples of all nations, baptizing them in the name of the Father and of the Son and of the Holy Spirit, [20]and teaching them to obey everything that I have commanded you. And remember, I am with you always, to the end of the age."

### *John 1:1–5, 9–14, 16–18*

[1]In the beginning was the Word, and the Word was with God, and the Word was God. [2]He was in the beginning with God. [3]All things came into being through him, and without him not one thing came into being. What has come into being [4]in him was life, and the life was the light of all people. [5]The light shines in the darkness, and the darkness did not overcome it. . . .

. . . [9]The true light, which enlightens everyone, was coming into the world.

[10]He was in the world, and the world came into being through him; yet the world did not know him. [11]He came to what was his own, and his own people did not accept him. [12]But to all who received him, who believed in his name, he gave power to become children of God, [13]who were born, not of blood or of the will of the flesh or of the will of man, but of God.

[14]And the Word became flesh and lived among us, and we have seen his glory, the glory as of a father's only son, full of grace and truth. . . . [16]From his fullness we have all received, grace upon grace. [17]The law indeed was given through Moses; grace and truth came through Jesus Christ. [18]No one has ever seen God. It is God the only Son, who is close to the Father's heart, who has made him known.

*John 8:52–59*

⁵²The Jews said to him, "Now we know that you have a demon. Abraham died, and so did the prophets; yet you say, 'Whoever keeps my word will never taste death.' ⁵³Are you greater than our father Abraham, who died? The prophets also died. Who do you claim to be?" ⁵⁴Jesus answered, "If I glorify myself, my glory is nothing. It is my Father who glorifies me, he of whom you say, 'He is our God,' ⁵⁵though you do not know him. But I know him; if I were to say that I do not know him, I would be a liar like you. But I do know him and I keep his word. ⁵⁶Your ancestor Abraham rejoiced that he would see my day; he saw it and was glad." ⁵⁷Then the Jews said to him, "You are not yet fifty years old, and have you seen Abraham?" ⁵⁸Jesus said to them, "Very truly, I tell you, before Abraham was, I am." ⁵⁹So they picked up stones to throw at him, but Jesus hid himself and went out of the temple.

*John 14:8–10*

⁸Philip said to him, "Lord, show us the Father, and we will be satisfied." ⁹Jesus said to him, "Have I been with you all this time, Philip, and you still do not know me? Whoever has seen me has seen the Father. How can you say, 'Show us the Father'? ¹⁰Do you not believe that I am in the Father and the Father is in me? The words that I say to you I do not speak on my own; but the Father who dwells in me does his works."

*Acts 4:7–12*

⁷When they had made the prisoners stand in their midst, they inquired, "By what power or by what name did you do this?" ⁸Then Peter, filled with the Holy Spirit, said to them, "Rulers of the people and elders, ⁹if we are questioned today because of a good deed done to someone who was sick and are asked how this man has been healed, ¹⁰let it be known to all of you, and to all the people of Israel, that this man is standing before you in good health by the name of Jesus Christ of Nazareth, whom you crucified, whom God raised from the dead. ¹¹This Jesus is

> 'the stone that was rejected by you, the builders;
>     it has become the cornerstone.'

¹²There is salvation in no one else, for there is no other name under heaven given among mortals by which we must be saved."

*Philippians 2:5–11*

[5]Let the same mind be in you that was in Christ Jesus,

> [6]who, though he was in the form of God,
>     did not regard equality with God
>     as something to be exploited,
> [7]but emptied himself,
>     taking the form of a slave,
>     being born in human likeness.
> And being found in human form,
>     [8]he humbled himself
>     and became obedient to the point of death—
>     even death on a cross.

> [9]Therefore God also highly exalted him
>     and gave him the name
>     that is above every name,
> [10]so that at the name of Jesus
>     every knee should bend,
>     in heaven and on earth and under the earth,
> [11]and every tongue should confess
>     that Jesus Christ is Lord,
>     to the glory of God the Father.

*Ronald J. Feenstra, "Incarnation," in* A Companion to Philosophy of Religion, *ed. Philip L. Quinn and Charles Taliaferro (Oxford: Blackwell, 1999), 532–33*

The New Testament generates the Christian claim that Jesus Christ is the divine Son of God who took on human flesh, becoming like us in every respect except sin. In one of the earliest New Testament writings, the apostle Paul, probably quoting an early Christian hymn, says that Christ Jesus, though he was in the form of God, did not consider equality with God something to be clung to, but emptied himself, taking the form of a servant, being born in human likeness (Philippians 2:5–11). The prologue of John (1:1–18) speaks of the Word, who was in the beginning with God and was God, through whom all things came into being, and who became flesh, lived among us, and made God known to us.

Scripture affirms Jesus Christ's divinity in at least five ways. First, despite the biblical affirmation that there is but one God (Deuteronomy 6:4), Jesus Christ is referred to as God (Hebrews 1:8, John 1:1, 18), as Lord (1 Corinthians 8:6, Philippians 2:11), as "our great God and Savior" (Titus 2:13; cf. 2 Peter 1:1), and even as "My Lord and my God" (John 20:28). In addition, the Gospel of John frequently uses "I am", the Old Testament name of God, to refer to Jesus Christ (6:20; 8:24, 28, 58; 10:7; 13:19; 18:5–8). Second, Jesus' equality and unity with God are indicated by his bearing the "exact imprint" of God's being (Hebrews 1:3) and being one with God (John 10:30, 17:22). The "whole fullness of deity" dwells bodily in him (Colossians 2:9). Third, Jesus does the works that God does, as creator (John 1:3, Colossians 1:16, Hebrews 1:10), sustainer of all things (Hebrews 1:3), destroyer of death (2 Timothy 1:10), forgiver of sins (Mark 2:5–11 and parallels), ruler (Philippians 2:10, Hebrews 1:8), and judge (Matthew 25:31–46). Fourth, worship and prayer are properly directed toward Jesus, thereby acknowledging his divinity (John 18:6, 1 Corinthians 16:22, Hebrews 1:6, Revelation 22:20). Fifth, Jesus' existence prior to creation is adumbrated. Some passages leave the matter unsettled, speaking of Jesus as "the image of the invisible God, the firstborn of all creation" (Colossians 1:15), or as the firstborn, begotten of the Father (Hebrews 1:5–6), or even as having existed before Abraham did (John 8:58). Nevertheless, John 1:1–2 indicates that the Word existed with God prior to creation, and the book of Revelation (1:17, 2:8, 22:13) ascribes to Jesus the divine title of "the first and the last".

The New Testament also affirms Jesus' humanity and his sharing in our temptations and limitations. Jesus' humanity is evident in his having become flesh, being born in human form (John 1:14; Philippians 2:7), his having eaten with his disciples, his thirst (John 19:28), and his death from crucifixion. Having become like us, he "in every respect has been tempted as we are, yet without sin", so he can sympathize with our weaknesses (Hebrews 2:17–18; 4:15). His having had limited knowledge is implied by statements that he grew in wisdom (Luke 2:52), learned obedience through what he suffered (Hebrews 5:8), wondered who touched him and received healing (Mark 5:30–3), and claimed not to know the day or hour that heaven and earth will pass away (Mark 13:32).

Given the biblical statements regarding Jesus Christ, Christians must affirm both his divinity, despite objections that no divine person could have been human or tempted or non-omniscient, and his humanity, despite objections that no human being could have pre-existed or been divine.

*Morna D. Hooker, "Chalcedon and the New Testament," in* The Making and Remaking of Christian Doctrine, *ed. Sarah Coakley and David A. Pailin (Oxford: Clarendon Press, 1993), 76–79, 81, 86–88, 90*

I suspect that Paul took it for granted that Christ was pre-existent, though until we get to Colossians (which may or may not have been written by Paul himself) there is little sign of any interest in what he did in his pre-existence. Christ represents God's purpose for mankind, and he is certainly no afterthought or addition to the plan: he must therefore have been from the beginning. But pre-existence does not necessarily imply divinity. I believe that it was in fact in thinking out Christ's relationship with the Law that the idea of pre-existence became important. It is suggestive that the first indication of Christ's pre-existence (1 Cor. 8:6) speaks of him as the one through whom creation exists—a role attributed in Jewish thought to the Law (*Midr. Rab. Gen.* 1.1). It would take us too far afield to explore Paul's teaching on the Law in any detail: suffice it to say that in Paul's understanding of the relationship between God and his people there is a sense in which Christ replaces the Law; or rather, since Paul insists that his teaching *establishes* the Law, the Law is discovered to be a temporary dispensation which points forward to the finality which is revealed in Christ. Compared with Christ, the Law is a kind of rough first draft—an inadequate metaphor, since it suggests that God found it necessary to have several attempts before producing the perfect version. And this, of course, is precisely where the idea of pre-existence comes in, for in Jewish thinking the Law was pre-existent—inevitably, because it expressed God's will for his people. If Christ has taken over from the Law, and is found to represent God's will for his people even more profoundly than the Law, then of course he must be pre-existent also; the Law is not so much a first draft as a somewhat blurred xerox copy, whereas Christ is the perfect image. Christ is thus greater than the Law: he embodies God's will for his people more completely than the Law; moreover, what the Law could not do God has now done, working through Christ—namely, recreated mankind in the image and likeness of God. . . .

But this means, of course, that everything that happens through Christ is the activity of God himself. To use Paul's classic phrase: "God was in Christ, reconciling the world to himself" (2 Corinthians 5:19). Thus when the disobedience of the one man Adam is weighed against the obedience of the one man Christ in Romans 5, the scales come down heavily on the side of Christ, who is a better man than Adam, precisely because the grace of God is at work through him. Because Christ is Son of God, truly obedient to God's will, the power of God is channelled through him. He stands over against the rest of humanity, even though he is one with them. Moreover, the same set of terms serves at one and the same time to identify him both as one with God and as one with mankind. We have already listed the language which Paul uses in speaking of Christ as the true Adam: he is Son of God; in the form of God; the image of God; Lord. This is language which *we* consider more appropriate for expressing what we would term Christ's "divinity". For Paul, these terms express the fact that Christ is one with God, precisely because they express his obedience as man. But because he speaks in terms of activity, rather than in terms of being, he thinks of Christ as one with God in purpose and will, rather than in nature. . . .

Thus it would seem that statements which appear at first sight to be "incarnational formulae" are not, strictly speaking, "incarnational" at all. Rather, for Paul, they refer to the conviction that by sharing our fallen humanity (i.e. life in Adam) Christ enabled men and women to become what he is: but Paul does not, as did Athanasius, understand that as meaning that they become divine. . . . Paul's use of the pattern of "interchange" suggests that he understands Christ's willing identification with our fallen humanity to be balanced by our resultant identification with his true humanity. If we use the term "incarnation" of the statement that "he became what we are", then what word are we to use of the balancing statement that we in turn become what he is? It is better to speak of "Second Adam" christology: a new creation has taken place, and humanity has been redeemed through one who is (in Luther's phrase) "proper Man." . . .

Ought we, then, to speak of John's understanding of Jesus in terms of a doctrine of "God incarnate"? After all, he declares in 1:1 that "the Word was God"; in 1:18 he speaks of Jesus, according to what may well be the correct reading, as *monogenes theos* [*only God*]. Moreover, at the end of the gospel he has Thomas confess Jesus as "my Lord and my God". Is this not what we understand as "incarnation"?

I think not. I suspect that it is misleading to use that term because it disguises the very different frames of reference within which our evangelist, on the one hand, and the Fathers of the Church, on the other, were working. It is worth noting how, in each of these three instances, John also makes it quite clear that the Word, or Jesus, stands over against God. Thus in 1:1 the declaration that the Word was God is sandwiched in between two statements that "The Word was *with* God." Whether or not 1:18 does in fact describe Jesus as "only God" (rather than as "only Son"), this comment follows a declaration that "No one has ever seen God." And though in 20:28 the risen Jesus is acknowledged by Thomas as "my Lord and my God", Jesus himself, a few verses earlier, declares that he is ascending "to my Father and your Father, to my God and your God". Similarly, in the rest of the Gospel, though we find Jesus proclaiming "Before Abraham was, I am" (8:58), he also declares "My Father is greater than I" (14:28). The relationship between Father and Son is one of dependence on the Son's part: "the Son can do nothing of his own accord, but only what he sees the Father doing" (5:19); "My teaching is not mine, but his who sent me" (7:16). Though the term "Son" is much more common in the Fourth Gospel than in Paul, its function is similar. . . .

This brief survey of some of the more significant christological statements in the New Testament will perhaps explain why I feel that there is a great gulf between the thought-world in which they were fashioned and that which gave rise to the Chalcedonian definition [*the two-natures Christology accepted by the church at the Council of Chalcedon in 451; see section 1.4*]. Though it is easy to see how the sayings of the Fourth Gospel came to be interpreted in terms of "incarnation", none of our writers was in fact describing "how God became man". Moreover, those passages in the Pauline epistles and in Hebrews which seem to us like references to "incarnation" are in fact concerned primarily to express the purpose of God for humanity, now fulfilled in Christ. Let me sum up by suggesting three reasons why the language of Chalcedon is so different from that of the New Testament.

First of all, Chalcedon was primarily intended as a bastion against heresy. Definition was necessary in order to make quite clear which heretical views were being excluded. In the days of the New Testament, on the other hand, Christianity was itself the heresy. This is something which is frequently forgotten by exegetes, who tend to read back later situations into the New Testament and suppose that our writers were defending the true Christian gospel against this or that heresy. But for most of the time they were not; they were propagating a message which was itself heretical, and were still in the process of working out its significance. The orthodoxy was Judaism; the Christian sect was trying to work out its position *vis-à-vis* the parent body and to reconcile faith in Jesus as God's Messiah with the conviction that God was indeed the God who had revealed himself to his people in the past. What our writers say about Christ has to be seen in this context. By the time of the Chalcedonian Council, the statements which had once been heresy had become orthodoxy, and were therefore handled in a completely different way.

Secondly, our New Testament writers were primarily concerned about describing the activity of God: he had acted, he had redeemed his people. They used a great variety of imagery—anything and everything available to them—in order to describe this activity; it was natural to them to employ narrative and metaphor. Their concern was not to offer definitions of the being of God or the being of Christ. The nature of God is known by what he does: many of the most important New Testament christological passages are hymns extolling God for what he has done through Christ. This is what is meant by describing New Testament christology as "functional" rather than as "ontological"; it seems to me to be a valid distinction. Nor is this simply an aberration on the part of our New Testament writers: it is part of the biblical tradition. Nowhere in the Old Testament does one find God being spoken of in terms of pure being: even in Deutero-Isaiah, where the description of God is at its most majestic, God is still celebrated as the one who acts. He is the God who reveals himself to his people and acts on their behalf, "the God of Abraham, Isaac and Jacob", the "Lord your God, who brought you out of the land of Egypt" (Exod. 3:6; 20:2). But by the time of Chalcedon things had changed radically; after four centuries in which Christians had grown accustomed to the idea of a divine Father and a divine Son and were used to speaking of them as peers, the Fathers of the Church approached the questions of christology in a very different way. . . . What had been for our New Testament authors helpful images used to describe their experience of God have now become doctrines which themselves need to be defined and analysed.

Thirdly, leading on from there, our New Testament authors write from within a Jewish context and not a Greek philosophical one. One hesitates these days to make contrasts between Greek and Hebrew language, but in spite of the pitfalls involved in easy contrasts it is still true to say that there are differences in outlook. Paul, for example, could never have spoken of Christ as "consisting of a reasonable soul and a body". He speaks of man as *soma psuchikon*, and the contrasts he uses are not between God and man, but between spirit and flesh. The debate at Chalcedon makes no sense to those accustomed to think in Jewish terms. Most important of all, the issues were quite different: our New Testament authors were wrestling with the question: "How do our new beliefs about Christ relate to what we have always believed about God—about the creation of the universe, his election of Israel, and his promises to his people?" Their concern was to show that it was the same God who had been at work in the past who was now at work in Christ, and that his new work in Christ was the fulfilment of everything that had gone before: hence the importance of showing his superiority to Moses.

The idea of an incarnate God is, we suggest, foreign to Jewish thinking. . . .

One of the false assumptions that has often confused the debate is the belief that the kind of interpretation of the New Testament evidence which we have been giving is of a "low" christology, in contrast to the "high" christology which focuses on incarnation. But it would be quite wrong to suppose that what we have discovered in the New Testament is a "low" christology. Our New Testament writers are convinced that God acts through Christ, that he speaks through him, and that he reveals himself in him. They use terms which are dynamic rather than metaphysical, but in their own way they express the conviction that in Christ they have "seen" God. To insist that the New Testament should be read in its own terms is in no sense to advocate a "reductionist" christology. It is not a question of "high" and "low," but rather of *different* christologies, worked out in totally different thought-worlds in answer to different problems: to judge one in terms of the other and to find it wanting is to misunderstand what is taking place.

*Larry W. Hurtado*, Lord Jesus Christ
*(Grand Rapids: Eerdmans, 2003), 649–51*

I contend that what we have examined in these chapters, "earliest Christianity" (ca. 30–170), provided the major convictions, and the parameters of belief and devotional practice as well, that shaped the subsequent developments in Christian tradition, which in turn came to be dominant and which form our picture of classical Christian faith. The devotional practice of earliest Christianity was particularly foundational for doctrinal developments. Though beliefs, or at least fundamental convictions, were certainly there from the outset, what followed was also heavily prompted, and decisively shaped, in the light of earliest Christian devotional practice.

Christians were proclaiming and worshiping Jesus, indeed, living and dying for his sake, well before the doctrinal/creedal developments of the second century and thereafter that have received so much attention in histories of Christian tradition. The early convictions about Jesus and the corresponding devotion offered to him that became so widespread in earliest Christianity were sufficiently robust to nourish the prolonged and vigorous efforts to articulate Christian faith in persuasive doctrinal formulations.

Moreover, devotion to Jesus as divine erupted suddenly and quickly, not gradually and late, among first-century circles of followers. More specifically, the origins lie in Jewish Christian circles of the earliest years. Only a certain wishful thinking continues to attribute the reverence of Jesus as divine decisively to the influence of pagan religion and the influx of Gentile converts, characterizing it as developing late and incrementally. Furthermore, devotion to Jesus as the "Lord," to whom cultic reverence and total obedience were the appropriate response, was widespread, not confined or attributable to particular circles, such as "Hellenists" or Gentile Christians of a supposed Syrian "Christ cult."

Amid the diversity of earliest Christianity, belief in Jesus' divine status was amazingly common. The "heresies" of earliest Christianity largely presuppose the view that Jesus is divine. That is not the issue. The problematic issue, in fact, was whether a genuinely *human* Jesus could be accommodated. Especially in the second century, "proto-orthodox" Christianity comprised those circles that regarded Jesus' human life as crucial in making his redemptive work efficacious.

Additionally, in spite of the diversity, it is equally evident that Jesus was *central* in all the forms of earliest Christianity, proto-orthodox or others, that we can describe with any confidence. This centrality of Jesus, and the uniqueness of his status in the various religious convictions of earliest Christians, also demanded, almost unavoidably, a new view of God.

. . . In the second century, however, there were a few competing options on what view of God was to be widely embraced as best representing what Christians should confess. [*The examples that follow are all versions of what came to be known as Gnosticism.*] For example, was Jesus to be seen as an emanation from the divine *plērōma* (the "All"), from which the elect themselves had been separated? Was Jesus the representative of a hitherto unknown, alien God who was not to be associated with the creator deity of the Old Testament? Was it in fact totally inappropriate to link the God from whom Jesus came with this world, creation, and bodily existence? Or was the Christian God properly to be identified as the Old Testament deity who had created all things, had spoken truly through Moses and the prophets, and now was revealed more fully and decisively through Jesus?

The last option was, of course, the one espoused by what I have called "proto-orthodox Christianity," and this constellation of Christians (who, to be sure, exhibited a certain variety of emphases and outlooks) developed across the period of our analysis what amounted to a new and unique view of what the term "God" meant. Granted, they drew freely upon Jewish tradition, as reflected in their insistence that the one God was prop-

erly thought of as a personal deity of love, purpose, justice, and faithfulness. The influence of Jewish tradition was also reflected in their critique
of pagan polytheism. Furthermore, like their Jewish coreligionists, they
came to draw selectively upon philosophical traditions; but in the earliest
centuries they did so with considerable caution.

The sum of proto-orthodox Christian teaching about God, however,
included critically new elements. Although they stridently professed sole
allegiance to the God of the Old Testament, their exclusivist monotheism
sometimes being tested by the threat of death, they also posited a real and
radical plurality, initially more focused on the "Father" and "Son", as
somehow pertaining to the one God they worshiped to the exclusion of
all others. That is, earliest Christian faith in Jesus contributed to a literal
reshaping of the monotheism inherited from the Jewish/biblical tradition,
initially taking things in a "binitarian" direction, though a trinitarian
model subsequently became dominant. I emphasize, also, that this reshaping of belief about God was accompanied and expressed by a corresponding "binitarian" pattern of devotional practice, in which the exalted Jesus
was included as recipient of reverence along with God "the Father."

The struggle to work out doctrinal formulations that could express in
some coherent way this peculiar view of God (as "one" and yet somehow
comprising "the Father" and Jesus, thereafter also including the Spirit as
the "third Person" of the Trinity) occupied the best minds in early Christian orthodox/catholic tradition for the first several centuries. But the
doctrinal problem they worked on was not of their making. It was forced
upon them by the earnest convictions and devotional practice of believers from the earliest observable years of the Christian movement.

*Andrew Chester,* Messiah and Exaltation *(Tübingen: Mohr Siebeck, 2007),*
*13, 14, 16–17, 18–19, 27, 29–30, 36, 119–20*

I see the essential difference as whether very high or incarnational Christology is a phenomenon utterly alien and unacceptable to first-century
Judaism, and needs a decisively non-Jewish context in order for this altogether different form to be able to emerge; or whether it represents a
development that is intelligible within a Palestinian Jewish context, and is
indeed possible only within that context, however much it represents
something extraordinary and unique in relation to what we find in Judaism
otherwise. . . .

. . . Casey argues that "it took 50 or 60 years to turn a Jewish prophet
into a Gentile God" [M. Casey, *From Jewish Prophet to Gentile God: The*

*Origins and Development of New Testament Christology* (Cambridge: James Clarke; Louisville, KY: Westminster John Knox Press, 1991), 97]. In order for this to happen, early Christianity had to evolve through stages: first, as fully Jewish, then with Gentiles entering the Christian community in significant numbers, without becoming Jewish, and thirdly and finally, where Christianity is identifiable as a Gentile religion. . . .

. . . At the very least [Casey] alerts us to issues that we should really not need reminding of: that Jesus was, whatever else, very much a first-century Palestinian Jew, and that what the New Testament affirms about Christ raises, in acute form, questions about its compatibility with Jewish monotheism.

The first of these themes has been strongly reinforced by Vermes in his latest book on Jesus, itself representing and developing further the main thrust of his earlier work in this area (G. Vermes, *The Changing Faces of Jesus*, London, Penguin, 2000; cf. also *idem, Jesus the Jew: A Historian's Reading of the Gospels*, London, SCM, 2nd edition, 1983; *idem, The Religion of Jesus the Jew*, London, SCM, 1993; and cf. also *idem, Jesus and the World of Judaism*, London, SCM, 1983). Thus he sets himself to uncover the real Jesus, who can still be detected in the Synoptic Gospels as an exceptional first-century Palestinian charismatic healer and exorcist, and a teacher and prophet proclaiming the Kingdom of God, from beneath the overlay of secondary interpretation that culminates in the portrayal of an altogether divine Christ in John's Gospel. Whatever we make of this essentially evolutionary account of New Testament Christology, both overall and in detail, we should be grateful for the compelling portrait of the genuinely Jewish Jesus who is at the heart of the Gospel accounts, and never lose sight of this. . . .

Bauckham deliberately argues for a radically different understanding of New Testament Christology in relation to first-century Jewish monotheism (R. Bauckham, *God Crucified: Monotheism and Christology in the New Testament*, Carlisle, Paternoster, 1998). This Judaism had unique ways of characterizing the unique identity of God, and the early Christians included Jesus precisely and unambiguously in this identity. They did so, however, not on the analogy of . . . intermediary figures (angelic and human). . . . It was a strict monotheism, with an absolute boundary between the one God and all created reality. Hence the so-called intermediary figures could not be understood as semi-divine or as straddling the boundary between God and creation: they either belonged fully within the divine identity or not at all. Most did not belong, and were seen as being unambiguously creatures. Wisdom and Logos (and Spirit), by contrast, are personifications or hypostatizations of God, are intrinsic to the unique divine identity, and again therefore do not compromise this in any way. Thus the distinction between belonging and not belonging within the divine identity is absolute, and it is simply not possible to move gradually into this divine identity through a series of stages. . . . On the contrary, New Testament Christology is already a full divine Christology, with Christ as intrinsic to the unique and eternal identity of God. . . .

The understanding of Christ as divine, on [Bauckham's] argument, certainly belongs fully within a Jewish context and at a very early stage, but it in no sense represents a development. . . .

Eskola sees Merkabah mysticism as centrally important for the understanding of New Testament Christology, but at the same time he sees this Christology itself as in need of a distinctively new approach (T. Eskola, *Messiah and the Throne*, Tübingen, Mohr Siebeck, 2001). [*Merkabah mysticism is Jewish mysticism that focuses on the divine "throne-chariot" of Ezekiel, and was known at Qumran and elsewhere.*] He takes over Scholem's definition of Merkabah mysticism as "above all throne mysticism," that is, with description of the heavenly palace and God sitting on the heavenly throne, and with the palace portrayed as a divine temple. . . .

. . . New Testament Christology uses the main aspects of Merkabah mysticism, and has the same symbolic world as Jewish apocalyptic: that is, portraying God as a theocratic king, with a heavenly court, and even temple, and a divine throne of Glory. The book of Acts, especially, provides very important evidence for this enthronement and exaltation discourse (especially Acts 2:22–36; cf. Psalms 16, 110, 132). . . .

Thus the resurrected Jesus is exalted as the Davidic messiah on the throne of Glory in heaven. There is a clear dependence on Merkabah mysticism, and this helps explain why enthronement on the heavenly throne of Glory, set centrally, was necessary for Jewish Christian Christology. Extraordinarily, however, the ascent and Merkabah speculation are here applied to a Davidic messiah and historical figure. . . . There is some evidence, in Jewish theology and mysticism, for the highest figures in the heavenly world being designated "gods", and having a soteriological function, but there is no analogy at all for applying these to a historical figure. . . . What this suggests is not an adoptionist concept, but that the enthroned one would have had deified status already. The same basic exaltation Christology is also found in Acts 5:30–31 and Acts 7. . . .

. . . The status of God himself, however, is *not* changed; what is new is the unique status of Christ, now identified as the divine ruler on God's throne. This early Christology is a radical intertextual transformation, where the tradition is completely at the service of the new message. . . .

. . . There are very important similarities between early Christianity and Judaism, yet at the same time . . . it needs to be perceived that early

Christianity's position, above all as far as Christology is concerned, is utterly and absolutely distinct. To hold these together simultaneously is a very difficult and precarious balancing act. Casey . . . resolves this question by arguing that early Christianity only developed its distinctive and absolute position when it had moved completely *outside* Judaism. Bauckham also resolves this question decisively, but by a radically different method. That is, Christ is seen as fully divine from the start, and has nothing whatever to [do] with the characteristic and distinctive Jewish categories (either angelic or human) that appear to belong closely in relation to God. Eskola sets early Christianity and Christology much more centrally within Judaism, but uses discourse analysis, and related methods, to show it to be utterly different, even (indeed, precisely) where it seems to have most in common.

These different approaches are all illuminating, and all take us further and more deeply into the main significant issues and evidence. Yet they all in the end have to be judged unsatisfactory; indeed, they all, in one way or another, set up a false antithesis. My own argument, over against the positions they variously represent, is that the phenomenon of earliest Christology can only be understood as developing within a Jewish context, and that Jewish intermediary figures constitute a central and integral part of that context. It is not the case, however, that earliest Christology can be explained by a simple correlation between Jesus and any of these figures. Nor is it possible to see a straightforward causal connection leading from these kinds of Jewish figures to exalted portrayals of Christ. The traditions about these Jewish figures do, however, show them mediating and moving between the heavenly and earthly, and divine and human, spheres. They also show us that the barrier between these spheres is becoming (increasingly) permeable. In a number of these traditions we also find striking portrayals of human figures, in a visionary context, being transformed into more than human appearance—at times indeed, it would seem, into more than angelic form—and in some cases set alongside God in the heavenly world.

Hence I have argued that it is the early Christian visionary experiences of the resurrected Jesus, as transformed and set alongside God in the heavenly world, that are crucially important for the development of Christology. These experiences could be understood and interpreted within the framework of Jewish visionary traditions of transformation. And what happens in the case of those figures who are transformed within these traditions would enable the early Christians to at least begin to be able to make sense of what has happened in the case of Jesus, and how he is to be understood. Yet these visionary traditions in themselves do not provide a sufficient explanation for the phenomenon of earliest Christology. They do not as such allow the early Christians to speak of Jesus as divine, and in any case, it is utterly without precedent to see a contemporary human figure (all the more so, in the case of one who has been executed as a criminal) taking on exalted form, and being set alongside God in the heavenly world. Nor can the claim that Jesus has been raised from the dead in itself give rise to that kind of understanding of him, even though it would allow him to be set within the heavenly world in more general terms.

It is, then, necessary here to take account also of how Jesus is perceived within his lifetime: of what he says and does, and how he appears to stand in relation to God. Here certainly, as I have argued, Jesus' own visionary experiences, and the visionary experience others have of him within his lifetime, will have been centrally important in enabling the early Christians to make the claims they do about him. Yet the point that needs to be insisted on is that these experiences are only able to have this effect when set in conjunction with what is known otherwise of Jesus: his proclaiming of the Kingdom of God, his inaugurating of this, especially in his healing and exorcising, and the intimate relationship of sonship with God that he had claimed to have.

## 1.2 The Creation of the Classic Creed

*Over a period of time the creed that we now know as the Nicene Creed was gradually agreed upon. In 325, the emperor Constantine, who had recently converted to Christianity, summoned the first ecumenical ("universal") council of the church to meet at Nicaea, very near his own new imperial capital of Constantinople (Byzantium, modern Istanbul). He wanted to see a strong, united church instead of the disunity that then existed between those who thought of Christ as the Father's equal and those like Arius (c. 250–336) who thought of him as first-born of all creation, and therefore that there was a time when he did not exist. The nonbiblical term* homoousios *was used to assert Christ's equality (for ambiguities in the meaning of the term, see "*homoousios*" in the Glossary of Christological Terms). The creed was then expanded at a second council in 381 to accord the same status to the Holy Spirit.*

*The Creed of Nicaea*
*From the Council of Nicaea, 325*
*(trans. Henry Bettenson, in his* Documents of the Christian Church
*[London: Oxford University Press, 1963], 25)*

We believe in one God the Father All-sovereign, maker of all things visible and invisible;

And in one Lord Jesus Christ, the Son of God, begotten of the Father, only-begotten, that is, of the substance of the Father, God of God, Light of Light, true God of true God, begotten not made, of one substance with the Father, through whom all things were made, things in heaven and things on the earth; who for us men and for our salvation came down and was made flesh, and became man, suffered, and rose on the third day, ascended into the heavens, is coming to judge living and dead.

And in the Holy Spirit.

And those that say "There was when he was not,"

and, "Before he was begotten he was not,"

and that, "He came into being from what-is-not,"

or those that allege, that the son of God is

"Of another substance or essence"

or "created,"

or "changeable"

or "alterable,"

these the Catholic and Apostolic Church anathematizes.

*The Nicaeno-Constantinopolitan Creed*
*From the Council of Constantinople, 381*
*(Epiphanius,* Ancoratus, *118, trans. Henry Bettenson,* Documents of the Christian Church *[London: Oxford University Press, 1963], 26)*

We believe in one God the Father All-sovereign, maker of heaven and earth, and of all things visible and invisible;

And in one Lord Jesus Christ, the only-begotten Son of God, Begotten of the Father before all the ages, Light of Light, true God of true God, begotten not made, of one substance with the Father, through whom all things were made; who for us men and for our salvation came down from the heavens, and was made flesh of the Holy Spirit and the Virgin Mary, and became man, and was crucified for us under Pontius Pilate, and suffered and was buried, and rose again on the third day according to the Scriptures, and ascended into the heavens, and sitteth on the right hand of the Father, and cometh again with glory to judge living and dead, of whose kingdom there shall be no end:

And in the Holy Spirit, the Lord and the Life-giver, that proceedeth from the Father, who with Father and Son is worshipped together and glorified together, who spake through the prophets:

In one holy Catholic and Apostolic Church:

We acknowledge one baptism unto remission of sins. We look for a resurrection of the dead, and the life of the age to come.

*An Argument of Athanasius against the Arians (c. 358)*
(Contra Arianos, *2.31, trans. Henry Bettenson, in his* The Early Christian Fathers *[London: Oxford University Press, 1969], 283)*

*The Arians maintained that the Son was not the equal of the Father.*

The Word of God was not made for us; rather we were made for him and "in him all things were created" [Colossians 1:16]. Nor is it true that because of our weakness he, the strong, was brought into being by the Father (who then existed alone), in order that he might fashion us through him as by an instrument. Nothing could be further from the truth! For even if God had decided not to make created things, still the Word would have been "with God" none the less, and the Father in him. While created things could not have come into being without the Word . . . For as the light enlightens all things with its radiance, and without that radiance nothing would be illuminated, so the Father wrought all things through the Word, as by a hand. For instance, God said, "Let there be light" [Genesis 1:3]. . . . And he did not speak in order that some subordinate might hear, understand what the speaker wanted, and go and perform the task. This is what happens in human affairs. But the Word of God is creator and maker, and he *is* the Father's will.

[*Such views came to define orthodoxy ("right belief"), over against heresy (derived from the Greek word for "choice"), which was seen as representing a personal theology as against the agreed corporate view.*]

### 1.3 Early Debates over Christ's Humanity

*Gregory of Nazianzus*
*An Examination of Apollinarianism (c. 380–81)*
(Letters, *101, trans. Henry Bettenson,* Documents of the Christian Church *[London: Oxford University Press, 1963], 45)*

*One of the so-called Cappadocian Fathers, Gregory (329–c. 390) was made bishop in 372. He was a defender of orthodoxy against Apollinarius (c. 310–90), who had become bishop of Laodicaea around 360. "Apollinarianism," the heresy that bears his name, is the belief that in Christ the Word took the place of his human soul. The unity of the person was thus preserved, but at the cost of an incomplete humanity.*

Do not let men deceive themselves and others by saying that . . . "Our Lord and God" is without a human mind. We do not separate the Man from the Deity, no, we assert the dogma of the unity and identity of the Person, who aforetime was not man but God, the only Son before all ages, who in these last days has assumed manhood also for our salvation; in his flesh passible, in his Deity impassible; in the body circumscribed, uncircumscribed in the Spirit; at once earthly and heavenly, tangible and intangible, comprehensible and incomprehensible; that by one and the same person, perfect man and perfect God, the whole humanity, fallen through sin, might be created anew.

If any one does not believe that holy Mary is the mother of God, he is cut off from the Deity. . . . If any assert that the manhood was fashioned and afterwards endued with the Deity, he also is to be condemned. . . . If any bring in the idea of two sons, one of God the Father, the other of the mother, may he lose his share in the adoption. . . . For the Godhead and the manhood are two natures, as are soul and body, but there are not two sons or two Gods. . . . For both natures are one by the combination, the Godhead made man or the manhood deified, or whatever be the right expression. . . .

If any one has put his trust in him as a man without a human mind, he is himself devoid of mind and unworthy of salvation. For what he has not assumed he has not healed; it is what is united to his Deity that is saved. . . . Let them not grudge us our entire salvation, or endue the saviour only with the bones and nerves and appearance of humanity.

*Theodore of Mopsuestia*, Catechetical Homilies 5
*(trans. Henry Bettenson, in his* The Later Christian Fathers
*[London: Oxford University Press, 1970], 166)*

*Theodore was one of the so-called Antiochene theologians. He was made bishop in 392, and died in 428.*

It was necessary that the Son should assume not only a body but also an immortal and rational soul. It was not only the death of the body that he had to abolish, but the death of the soul, which is sin. . . . It was necessary that sin, the cause of death, should be removed, and consequently death would be abolished with the removal of sin.

It is evident that the tendency to sin has its origin in the will of the soul. . . .

It was necessary, therefore, that Our Lord should take a soul, so that the soul should first be saved from sin and, by God's grace, should achieve immortality.

*Cyril of Alexandria,* Against the Blasphemies of Nestorius *2.10*
*(trans. Henry Bettenson, in* The Later Christian Fathers
*[London: Oxford University Press, 1970], 253–54)*

*Cyril (d. 444) was patriarch of Alexandria. Nestorius (d. 456) was an Anti-*
*ochene theologian who was made bishop of Constantinople in 428 and deposed in*
*431. Just as Apollinarius was seen as having pushed the Alexandrian stress on*
*Christ's divinity to an illegitimate extreme, so Nestorius was now accused of*
*allowing the Antiochene focus on Christ's humanity to threaten the unity of*
*Christ's identity as one person. The humanity, orthodoxy agreed, must not be*
*treated as a distinct person but as part of the one person that is Christ the Son*
*of God. (For ambiguities in the Greek for "person" upon which Nestorius plays,*
*see the glossary.)*

What I would say, my good Nestorius, is that although we speak of Christ
as man and at the same time God, we are not making a division in so speaking. Rather we knew this same Son and God and Word of the Father even
before his incarnation; and, after that, we knew him as made man, in our
condition, and incarnate. . . .

The division that he [Nestorius] makes is clear from his acknowledgement that worship is to be given *with* the divinity: for what is worshipped
*with* something else is surely quite distinct from that with which it is said
to be worshipped. But we are accustomed to worship Emmanuel with one
single worship, not separating from the Word the body which was personally united to him.

*Cyril of Alexandria, Letters 17*
*(trans. Henry Bettenson, Documents of the Christian Church*
*[London: Oxford University Press, 1963], 46)*

1. If any one does not acknowledge that Emmanuel is in truth God, and
that the holy Virgin is, in consequence, "Theotokos" ["*God-bearer*"], for
she brought forth after the flesh the Word of God who has become flesh,
let him be anathema.

2. If any one does not acknowledge that the Word which is from God the
Father was personally united with flesh, and with his own flesh is one Christ,
that is, one and the same God and man together, let him be anathema.

3. If any one in the one Christ divide the persons [*hypostaseis*] after their
union, conjoining them with a mere conjunction in accordance with
worth, or conjunction effected by authority or power, instead of a combination according to a union of natures, let him be anathema.

## 1.4 The Two-Natures Doctrine: Chalcedon, Its Interpretation, Defenses, and Opponents

*The Definition of Chalcedon*
*(trans. Henry Bettenson,* Documents of the Christian Church
*[London: Oxford University Press, 1963], 51–52)*

*The Definition of Chalcedon, agreed to at the Council of Chalcedon in 451, is regarded as the touchstone of christological orthodoxy.*

Therefore, following the holy Fathers, we all with one accord teach men to acknowledge one and the same Son, our Lord Jesus Christ, at once complete in Godhead and complete in manhood, truly God and truly man consisting also of a reasonable soul and body; of one substance [*homoousios*] with the Father as regards his Godhead, and at the same time of one substance with us as regards his manhood; like us in all respects, apart from sin; as regards his Godhead, begotten of the Father before the ages, but yet as regards his manhood begotten, for us men and for our salvation, of Mary the Virgin, the God-bearer [*theotokos*]; one and the same Christ, Son, Lord, Only-begotten, recognized IN TWO NATURES, WITHOUT CONFUSION, WITHOUT CHANGE, WITHOUT DIVISION, WITHOUT SEPARATION; the distinction of natures being in no way annulled by the union, but rather the characteristics of each nature being preserved and coming together to form one person and subsistence [*hypostasis*], not as parted or separated into two persons, but one and the same Son and Only-begotten God the Word, Lord Jesus Christ; even as the prophets from earliest times spoke of him, and our Lord Jesus Christ himself taught us, and the creed of the Fathers has handed down to us.

[*Not everyone accepted this definition, and in particular some churches in the East—which continue to this day—rejected the decision of the council. It was not until the twentieth century that they began to be more open to a positive reading of Chalcedon.*]

*R. A. Norris Jr., "Toward a Contemporary Interpretation of the Chalcedonian Definition," in* Lux in Lumine, *ed. R. A. Norris Jr.*
*(New York: Seabury Press, 1966), 76–79*

What our historical analysis suggests is that the *Definition*'s terminology can best be treated as *second-order language.* . . .

Interpreted in this sense, the Council's confession can be seen to assert at least four fundamental *dogmata*. First, and most obviously, it insists that all language which refers to Christ (that is, to the incarnate Word) is language about a single, individual subject. Such language does not characterize a class, or a collection, or an organic system of subjects. Sentences which make an assertion about Christ have the same logical character as descriptions or accounts of a particular person.

Second, the *Definition* lays it down that it is both possible and correct to talk about this subject in the same terms one would use to talk about an ordinary human person. Whatever categories of explanation and description are normally used to describe the appearance, the actions, and the words of a man may be used to give an account of the particular actions and words of Christ. Further, such an account of Christ is in principle *complete*. That is to say, all of the phenomena to which we refer when we speak of "Christ" can be described and understood by means of the same sort of language which we use about other men.

But third, the Council's confession demands that this same set of phenomena be described by use of the kind of language which men employ when they talk about God. The words and actions of Christ are to be understood by describing them and explaining them in terms which explicitly refer them to a divine source and characterize them as divine words and actions. Furthermore, this second way of giving an account of Christ must also be taken as in principle complete, in the sense which we have defined above.

Finally, the Council explains that these two ways of giving an account of Christ are not to be confused or equated with each other. They are logically different ways of talking about the same thing; and because both are necessary for an adequate Christian understanding of Christ, neither may be substituted for the other or assimilated to the other.

Obviously there is a sense in which these *dogmata* do not constitute a Christology. They merely specify, by means of a normative description of Christological language, what it is that a Christology sets out to understand and explain. Consequently it is merely wrongheaded to accuse the *Definition* of, for example, losing sight of the figure of the historical Jesus. The *Definition* is not talking about Jesus; it is talking about Christian language about Jesus. An adequate criticism of the Council's confession must address itself, therefore, to this problem, and ask about the clarity and adequacy of the position which the Fathers of Chalcedon took in their description of the logical form of Christological language. Here we can only suggest one or two lines of inquiry which seem to arise naturally out of this understanding of the nature of the Chalcedonian *Definition*.

The first and most obvious problem is that of the logical relation between the two ways of talking about Christ which the Council asserts to be *data* of Christian tradition. . . .

For modern theologians, therefore, the Chalcedonian *Definition* raises in a specific and acute form the question of the logical relation between language about God and "empirical" language. The *Definition* asserts that in the particular case of Christ these two kinds of language are both to be used to give an account of the same *explicandum*, yet that they are logically different and in some way mutually supplementary. Hence the question arises whether—and how—it can make sense to offer two different *kinds* of explanation of the very same event. This is the form which the problem of Christ's "natures" takes for modern theology.

The second difficulty is of a different sort. It arises out of a change in Christological perspective which has come about within the last two hundred years. The Fathers of Chalcedon agreed with Cyril of Alexandria and with a long tradition preceding him that the subject of statements about Christ was simply the divine Word. On the other hand, modern Christology conceives itself to be trying to understand Jesus of Nazareth in his birth, ministry, death, and resurrection.

*Sarah Coakley, "What Does Chalcedon Solve and What Does It Not? Some Reflections on the Status and Meaning of the Chalcedonian 'Definition,'" in* The Incarnation, *ed. Stephen T. Davis, Daniel Kendall, SJ, and Gerald O'Collins, SJ (Oxford: Oxford University Press, 2002), 160–63*

Let us now consider the crucial systematic issue touched on earlier, namely, whether and in what sense the "Definition" speaks "kataphatically" or "apophatically", and where the line is drawn between the two. [*"Kataphatic" theology allows a positive understanding of God, whereas "apophatic" theology asserts that God is not any of the things he is called.*] Here we shall, perforce, have finally to clarify what *genre* of text this is, and what we may appropriately expect of it.

An important clue here, I suggest, is provided by the very word used in Greek for the "Definition", that is, *horos*, or "horizon". The evocations are mostly not the same ones that are set off by the English "Definition"— that is, semantic clarity, linguistic precision, or careful circumscription (and we have already seen how Chalcedon apparently fails to deliver all of these). Rather, as a survey of the uses of *horos* in Lampe's *Patristic Lexicon* displays, meanings of *horos* in Greek range from "boundary", "horizon", and "limit", to "standard", "pattern", and (monastic) "rule". The word can also be used directly of Christ with the meaning of "expression" (Christ as the "*horos* and *logos* of God", in Gregory of Nazianzen). Thus, when it is also used of liturgical or dogmatic "decisions" and "decrees", it brings with it different semantic baggage from our English equivalent. . . .

Taking this semantic background into account, and remembering again that the assembled bishops at Chalcedon resisted at one point the Emperor's demand for greater "precision", we may perhaps begin to see the true intentions of the document. It does not, that is, intend to provide a full systematic account of Christology, and even less a complete and precise metaphysics of Christ's makeup. Rather, it sets a "boundary" on what can, and cannot, be said, by first ruling out three aberrant interpretations of Christ (Apollinarianism, Eutychianism, and extreme Nestorianism [*on Apollinarianism and Nestorianism, see pp. 19, 21; Eutychianism is the view that after the incarnation there was one single nature in Christ*]), second, providing an abstract rule of language (*physis* ["nature"] and *hypostasis* ["person"]) for distinguishing duality and unity in Christ, and, third, presenting a "riddle" of negatives by means of which a greater (though undefined) reality may be intimated. At the same time, it recapitulates and assumes (a point often forgotten in considering the *horos* in abstraction from the rest of the *Acta*) the acts of salvation detailed in Nicaea and Constantinople; and then it leaves us at that "boundary", understood as the place now to which those salvific acts must be brought to avoid doctrinal error, but without any supposition that this linguistic regulation thereby *explains* or *grasps* the reality towards which it points. In this, rather particular sense, it is an "apophatic" document.

What category or *genre* of text, then, is the Chalcedonian "Definition"? If my interpretation is right, it is clearly regulatory and binding as a "pattern" endorsed by an ecumenical council: reflections on Christ's person must henceforth pass through this "grid", as I put it at the outset. But it would be a mistake to expect it to deliver more than it can in its own terms, given its "apophatic" dimension. As Rahner puts it famously, it is "not end but beginning", or (more properly) "end *and* beginning". For the East, in any case, it has always represented one—albeit crucial—moment in a process of christological clarification that continued long afterwards, through the debates of the sixth and seventh centuries and up to and including the iconographical decrees of Nicaea II. [*This was the last ecumenical council of both East and West in 787, at which the legitimacy of images of Christ was finally accepted.*] From this perspective even Rahner is not quite modest enough in his ascription: Chalcedon is strictly speaking *neither* end *nor* beginning, but rather a transitional (though still normative) "horizon" to which we constantly return, but with equally constant forays backwards and forwards. Whereas the West has tended to "stop" at Chalcedon, and to expect of it something more metaphysically and substantially precise than it can yield, the East has in contrast tended to turn its phrases into liturgical prayer (especially in the *Theotokia* for Saturday Great Vespers), to gesture with it in worship beyond the "limit" that it sets. Endless ecumenical misunderstanding, of course, has resulted from this divergence.

It is worth enumerating, finally and in closing, some of the vital christological issues that Chalcedon *per se* cannot and does not solve. Not only is this undertaking suitably chastening, it also invites the last ecumenical reflection: is Chalcedon's "limit" regrettable or laudable?

Thus: (1) Chalcedon does not tell us in what the divine and human "natures" consist; (2) it does not tell us what *hypostasis* means when applied to Christ; (3) it does not tell us how *hypostasis* and *physeis* are related, or how the *physeis* relate to one another (the problem of the *communicatio idiomatum* [*the exchange of attributes between the two natures*]); (4) it does not tell us how many wills Christ has; (5) it does not tell us that the *hypostasis* is identical with the pre-existent Logos; (6) it does not tell us what happens to the *physeis* at Christ's death and in his resurrection; (7) it does not tell us whether the meaning of *hypostasis* in this christological context is different, or the same, from the meaning in the trinitarian context; (8) it does not tell us whether the risen Christ is male.

. . . The intriguing question that presses ecclesiologically for today is this: should *Chalcedon* be the primary bar of ecumenical engagement and discernment in christological matters? If so, its "apophatic" horizon (at least as I have propounded it) could shelter many more alternatives than later official clarifications, East and West, would appear to allow.

*Don Cupitt, "The Christ of Christendom," in* The Myth of God Incarnate, *ed. John Hick (London: SCM Press, 1993), 140, 142–43*

I believe that the way the dogma [of the incarnation] came to be defined had in the long run damaging effects upon belief in God, and upon the way man's relation to God was conceived. Four arguments will, I hope, make the point clear.

1. The assertion that deity itself and humanity are permanently united in the one person of the incarnate Lord suggests an ultimate synthesis, a conjunction and continuity between things divine and things of this

world. As the popular maxim had it, Grace does not destroy but perfects Nature.

This idea distorts Jesus' message. Christianity's proper subtlety and freedom depended upon Jesus' ironical perception of *disjunction* between the things of God and the things of men, a disjunction particularly enforced in the parables, as distinct from similitudes, allegories and analogies. Whether he is seen as an apocalyptic prophet or as a witty rabbi (or, as I think, both), what matters in Jesus' message is his sense of the abrupt juxtaposition of two opposed orders of things. The way things seem from one point of view is the opposite of the way they seem from the other. This emphasis on *contrasting* value-scales evokes the transcendent, and it underlies Jesus' paradoxes of righteousness and unrighteousness, loss and gain, death and life, poverty and riches, the manifest and the hidden, security and insecurity, prudence and folly, and justice and injustice. The essential thing is that the two contrasting orders must collide.

But the doctrine of the incarnation unified things which Jesus had kept in ironic contrast with each other. . . .

2. Orthodox doctrine asserts that the divine and the human are indissolubly united in the person of the divine Word, with effect from the moment of Christ's conception. This appears to assert that the union of God with man was miraculously accomplished by God independently of, because prior to, the struggles and suffering of Jesus' earthly life, which thus become peripheral. . . .

3. If in Jesus the fullness of God himself is permanently incarnate, Jesus can be directly worshipped as God without risk of error or blasphemy. A cult of Christ as distinct from a cult of God thus becomes defensible, and did in fact develop. The practice of praying direct to Christ in the Liturgy, as distinct from praying to God through Christ, appears to have originated among the innovating "orthodox" opponents of Arianism in the fourth century. It slowly spread, against a good deal of opposition, eventually to produce Christocentric piety and theology. An example of the consequent paganization of Christianity was the agreement to constitute the World Council of Churches upon the doctrinal basis of "acknowledgement of our Lord Jesus Christ as God and Saviour"—and nothing else. . . .

4. If it is the case that in the incarnation God himself has permanently assumed human nature, and can legitimately be depicted as God in human form, then eventually the ultimate mystery of deity will be conceived anthropomorphically, and the pagan notion of a deity as a superhuman

person with gender will be restored. In due course this happened, aided by the traditional Father-Son imagery.

*Herbert McCabe, OP,* God Matters
*(London: Geoffrey Chapman, 1987), 56–58, 60*

Part of the doctrine of the incarnation is precisely that Jesus was and is a human person; the other part is that this same identical person was and is divine. The adjectives "divine" and "human" express *what* Jesus is (his nature), the name "Jesus" refers to *who* (which person) he is. In virtue of his human nature certain things can be asserted or denied about Jesus; in virtue of his divine nature certain other things can be asserted or denied of him, but all these assertions are about one person. The point is a logical . . . one. . . . It is not, however, true to say "Jesus, *qua* God, died on the cross." . . . There is no special mystery about this: it is no more than the logical difference between saying "A policeman murdered his wife" and saying "Mr X, *qua* policeman, murdered his wife" . . .

. . . It is in this way that Chalcedon points to the mystery of Jesus. Let me repeat: we may well find other ways of articulating this mystery, but if we *are* to speak in these old-fashioned terms of essence, nature, person, then to deny the paradoxical proposition of Chalcedon is to fail to grasp in faith the mystery which is Jesus.

For Professor John Hick it is all rather simple: he writes as though no one had hitherto observed the oddness of ascribing two natures to Jesus. "For to say, without explanation, that the historical Jesus of Nazareth was also God is as devoid of meaning as to say that this circle drawn with a pencil on paper is also a square" [*The Myth of God Incarnate, 178*]. . . .

The mystery of Jesus is, like all mysteries, the mystery of what "God" means. If we are to explore it we shall have to explore what we can, and more particularly what we cannot, confidently assert concerning God. . . .

Circles and squares and triangles and such occupy their mutually exclusive territories in the common logical world of shapes. It is part of the *meaning* of a circle that it is not a square or any other shape; hence to say that something is both a circle and a square is to say both that it is and is not a circle, and this . . . is to say nothing at all. Similarly being human and being, say, a sheep occupy mutually exclusive territories in the common logical world of animals. It is part of the meaning of being human that one is not a sheep. And so on. But just what or where is the common logical world that is occupied in mutual exclusion by God and man? A circle and a square make two shapes; a man and a sheep make two animals:

God and man make two what? It may be part of the meaning of man that he is not any other creature; it cannot be part of the *meaning* of man that he is not God. God is not one of the items in some universe which have to be excluded if it is just man that you are talking about. God could not be an item in any universe.

It follows that there is not, after all, the same contradiction in saying that Jesus is both man and God as there would be in saying that a circle is a square or that Jesus is both man and sheep. This does not mean that we actually *understand* what it means to say that Jesus is man and God; of course we do not clearly understand this any more than we clearly understand what it means to say that God created the world or that the consecrated elements are the body and blood of Christ or indeed that God exists or that I am a sinner. The doctrine of the incarnation, like the doctrines of creation or redemption, is not conveying information, it is pointing to a mystery in Jesus. We require of such a doctrine not that it be clearly intelligible but that at least it should say something, i.e. that it should not contradict itself. This requirement, I think Professor Hick must on reflection agree, is satisfied by the doctrine of the incarnation.

*Maurice Wiles, "The Incarnation," in* God Matters, *ed. Herbert McCabe, OP (London: Geoffrey Chapman, 1987), 63–64*

In considering the issue of self-contradiction you [Herbert McCabe] reject John Hick's analogy of square and circle as too simple. I agree. The self-contradiction there is far clearer and more precise than in the case of God and man, because squares and circles are far clearer and more precise concepts. But your statement of the opposing case seems to me equally oversimplified. You write: "It may be part of the meaning of man that he is not any other creature; it cannot be part of the *meaning* of man that he is not God." Perhaps, but not self-evidently so. There is always an element of arbitrariness in deciding which characteristics of a species are part of its definition, part of the meaning of the term, and which are accidental corollaries, however unfailingly they appear. It seems to me not unreasonable to regard "being created" as part of the *meaning* of man (which there's no point in drawing attention to when what is at issue is the relation between man and other creatures) and "not being created" as part of the meaning of God. Now if there is an analogical relationship between God and man, if indeed there is any real relation between them (as you want strongly to insist), then they inhabit a common logical world, though not of course a common logical world of shapes. *Prima facie* at least there is a case of self-contradiction involved. I do not myself want to argue dog-matically that there is clear self-contradiction, but I am certainly not as clear as you appear to be that there is not. If I am to accept the doctrine as true and therefore also meaningful, I need convincing by some means other than simply reference to the Church's dogma. I want to know how the Church arrived at that conviction. And I want to be shown, not, I am ready to concede to you, that it is "clearly intelligible", but that it is the best way of making sense of all the evidence.

## Topics for Discussion

1. Does the biblical material all point in the same direction toward Christ's divinity, or do some passages allow a more human Jesus than others?

2. In defending Christ's divinity, to what is it most important to appeal—his actions, teaching, and titles, or the experience of the early disciples and their worship of him, or a combination of both? Can such assumptions be explained from the Jewish context alone?

3. In rejecting the heresies of Arius, Apollinarius, and Nestorius, what were the church fathers trying to preserve and defend? Did they succeed?

4. How should the decisions at Nicaea and Chalcedon be under-stood—as positive clarification, or as minimal restraints on what may or may not be said?

5. Does talk of God as a totally different kind of reality from the human lessen the sense of a logical puzzle, or is it likely only to add to the pressure from those (like Cupitt) who insist that to link two such unlike entities was always unstable?

*Chapter Two*

# Jesus of History or Christ of Faith?

## 2.1 The Problem Posed

*Paul Tillich*, Systematic Theology, *vol. 2*
*(London: Nisbet, 1957), 130–32, 134*

The preceding evaluation of the historical approach to the biblical records led to a negative and a positive assertion. The negative assertion is that historical research can neither give nor take away the foundation of the Christian faith. The positive assertion is that historical research has influenced and must influence Christian theology. . . .

But it is necessary systematically to raise once more a question which is continuously being asked with considerable religious anxiety. Does not the acceptance of the historical method for dealing with the source documents of the Christian faith introduce a dangerous insecurity into the thought and life of the church and of every individual Christian? Could not historical research lead to a complete scepticism about the biblical records? Is it not imaginable that historical criticism could come to the judgement that the man Jesus of Nazareth never lived? . . . It is inadequate to point out that historical research has not yet given any evidence to support such scepticism. Certainly, it has not yet! But the anxious question remains whether it could not do so sometime in the future! Faith cannot rest on such unsure ground. The answer, taken from the "not-yet" of sceptical evidence, is insufficient. There is another possible answer, which, though not false, is misleading. This is to say that the historical foundation of Christianity is an essential element of the Christian faith itself and that this faith, through its own power, can overrule sceptical possibilities within historical criticism. It can, it is maintained, guarantee the existence of Jesus of Nazareth and at least the essentials in the biblical picture. But we must analyse this answer carefully, for it is ambiguous. The problem is: Exactly what can faith guarantee? And the inevitable answer is that faith can guarantee only its own foundation, namely, the appearance of that reality which has created the faith. The reality is the New Being, who conquers existential estrangement and thereby makes faith possible. This alone faith is able to guarantee—and that because its own existence is identical with the presence of the New Being. . . .

. . . One must say that participation, not historical argument, guarantees the reality of the event upon which Christianity is based. It guarantees a personal life in which the New Being has conquered the old being. But it does not guarantee his name to be Jesus of Nazareth. Historical doubt concerning the existence and the life of someone with this name cannot be overruled. He might have had another name. (This is an historically absurd, but logically necessary, consequence of the historical method.) Whatever his name, the New Being was and is actual in this man.

But here a very important question arises. How can the New Being who is called "the Christ" transform reality if no concrete trait of his nature is left? Kierkegaard exaggerates when he says that it is sufficient for the Christian faith nakedly to assert that in the years 1–30 God sent his son. Without the concreteness of the New Being, its newness would be empty. Only if existence is conquered concretely and in its manifold aspects, is it actually conquered. The power which has created and preserved the community of the New Being is not an abstract statement about its appearance; it is the picture of him in whom it has appeared. No special trait of this picture can be verified with certainty. But it can be definitely asserted that through this picture the New Being has power to transform those who are transformed by it. This implies that there is an *analogia imaginis*, namely, an analogy between the picture and the actual personal life from which it has arisen. It was this reality, when encountered by the disciples, which created the picture. And it was, and still is, this picture which mediates the transforming power of the New Being. . . .

. . . The affirmation that Jesus is the Christ is an act of faith and consequently of daring courage. It is not an arbitrary leap into darkness but a decision in which elements of immediate participation and therefore certitude are mixed with elements of strangeness and therefore incertitude and doubt. But doubt is not the opposite of faith; it is an element of faith. Therefore, there is no faith without risk. The risk of faith is that it could affirm a wrong symbol of ultimate concern, a symbol which does not really express ultimacy (as, e.g., Dionysus or one's nation). But this risk lies in quite a different dimension from the risk of accepting uncertain historical facts. It is wrong, therefore, to consider the risk concerning uncertain historical facts as part of the risk of faith. The risk of faith is existential; it concerns the totality of our being, while the risk of historical judgements is theoretical and open to permanent scientific correction. Here are two different dimensions which should never be confused. A wrong faith can destroy the meaning of one's life; a wrong historical judgement cannot. It is misleading, therefore, to use the word "risk" for both dimensions in the same sense.

*Rudolf Bultmann,* Jesus and the Word, *trans. L. P. Smith and E. H. Lantero (London: Collins, 1958), 14–15*

*Interest in the personality of Jesus* is excluded—and not merely because, in the absence of information, I am making a virtue of necessity. I do indeed think that we can now know almost nothing concerning the life and personality of Jesus, since the early Christian sources show no interest in either, are moreover fragmentary and often legendary; and other sources about Jesus do not exist. Except for the purely critical research, what has been written in the last hundred and fifty years on the life of Jesus, his personality and the development of his inner life, is fantastic and romantic. Whoever reads Albert Schweitzer's brilliantly written *Quest of the Historical Jesus* must vividly realize this. The same impression is made by a survey of the differing contemporary judgements on the question of the Messianic consciousness of Jesus, the varying opinions as to whether Jesus believed himself to be the Messiah or not, and if so, in what sense, and at what point in his life. Considering that it was really no trifle to believe oneself Messiah, that, further, whoever so believed must have regulated his whole life in accordance with this belief, we must admit that if this point is obscure we can, strictly speaking, know nothing of the personality of Jesus. I am personally of the opinion that Jesus did not believe himself to be the Messiah, but I do not imagine that this opinion gives me a clearer picture of his personality. I have in this book not dealt with the question at all—not so much because nothing can be said about it with certainty as because I consider it of secondary importance.

However good the reasons for being interested in the personalities of significant historical figures, Plato or Jesus, Dante or Luther, Napoleon or Goethe, it still remains true that this interest does not touch that which such men had at heart; for *their* interest was not in their personality but in their *work.* And their work was to them not the expression of their personality, nor something through which their personality achieved its "form", but the cause to which they surrendered their lives. Moreover, their work does not mean the sum of the historical effects of their acts; for to this their view could not be directed. Rather, the "work" from *their* standpoint is the end they really sought, and it is in this connection with their purpose that they are the proper objects of historical investigation. This is certainly true if the examination of history is no neutral orientation about objectively determined past events, but is motivated by the question how we ourselves, standing in the current of history, can succeed in comprehending our own existence, can gain clear insight into the contingencies and necessities of our own life purpose.

In the case of those who like Jesus have worked through the medium of *word*, what they purposed can be reproduced only as a group of sayings, of ideas—as *teaching*. Whoever tries, according to the modern fashion, to penetrate behind the teaching to the psychology or to the personality of Jesus, inevitably, for the reasons already given, misses what Jesus purposed. For his purpose can be comprehended only as teaching.

*Van Austin Harvey,* The Historian and the Believer
*(London: SCM Press, 1967), 139–42, 146, 151–52*

[Bultmann] argues that the message of the New Testament is couched in a mythological language and that this message can be understood by modern men only if it is interpreted in a conceptual form that illuminates their own experience. The reason the mythological terms of the Bible must be translated into more intelligible forms, Bultmann believes, is not simply because modern man is no longer able to believe in a mythical world of supernatural beings who break into the nexus of history, but because the careful analysis of the use of mythology in the New Testament itself reveals that the intention of the Biblical writers is not to win assent to certain objective doctrines but to bring man to an authentic self-understanding, to a radical faith. The New Testament writers were primarily concerned to confront man with the self-destructiveness of trying to secure his existence on his own terms (to justify himself) and to proclaim to him the possibility of a new mode of existence (faith), an existence in which he finds his security in the unseen, in God. . . .

. . . One does not first believe that Jesus was divine and experience a liberation of the self; rather, by grasping the significance of the event one experiences a liberation of the self and calls Christ divine. . . .

There are, of course, many possible questions one can raise about Bultmann's position. But the one that concerns us here is this: If faith can be defined as a certain possibility of human existence which takes the form of self-surrender, in what sense is such a faith dependent on a past act of God in Jesus of Nazareth? Granted that the death and resurrection of Jesus provide a symbol embodying the true pattern of authentic existence in which the Christian participates, is it not possible that the same self-understanding might be gained in some other way by someone who had never heard of Jesus? Is not the faith that Bultmann describes a general human possibility? In what sense is the historical truth of the New Testament essential to faith when it is understood in this existentialist fashion? . . .

Bultmann's answer is equivocal. On the one hand, he argues that faith is no mysterious supernatural quality but simply the fulfilment of true human nature. It is a possibility that belongs to a man as man, a possibility for which he is accountable if he forfeits it. So, also, love is not "some mysterious supernatural power, but is man's 'natural' mode of relationship". On the other hand, Bultmann argues that faith and love are not human possibilities if by this we mean that one has only to know what they are and, then, to actualize them. They are made possible only by [a] prior act of God in Jesus Christ and in the *kerygma* about him. They can be achieved in no other way. . . .

A similar ambiguity hovers over the theology of Tillich. On the one hand, he develops in a powerful way a conception of faith which has affinities with the morality of knowledge and which, correspondingly, has little relation to the historical figure of Jesus of Nazareth or, for that matter, to any traditional Christian symbols. On the other hand, he insists that Christian faith is dependent on the actual life and death of Jesus of Nazareth. If the former conception enables Tillich to handle deftly the problems posed by historical research, the latter insistence brings those problems to the fore again and forces Tillich to engage in a tortured attempt to extricate himself from them. . . .

That Tillich does not wish to adopt Bultmann's solution seems quite clear, for he argues that the newness of the New Being would be empty without concreteness. . . .

One suspects that the real reason Tillich believes historical criticism can neither confirm nor deny the foundation of Christian faith is because the weight of his position finally rests on the New Testament picture of Jesus. It is really indifferent to Tillich whether this picture corresponds in any way to a past historical event. It is the picture of Jesus that conveys the power which grasps the religious imagination.

*The raising of such issues can be traced back to Schleiermacher (1768–1834),*
*who is often called the founder of modern theology because of the way in which he*
*places the primary stress on the human experience of Christ.*

*Friedrich Schleiermacher,* The Christian Faith, *trans. J. Y. Campbell*
*(Edinburgh: T. & T. Clark; New York: Charles Scribner's Sons, 1928), 387–88*

To ascribe to Christ an absolutely powerful God-consciousness, and to
attribute to Him an existence of God in Him, are exactly the same thing. . . .
. . . Just as the unconscious forces of nature and non-rational life become
a revelation of God to us only so far as we bring that conception with us, so
also that darkened and imperfect God-consciousness by itself is not an existence of God in human nature, but only in so far as we bring Christ with us
in thought and relate it to Him. So that originally it is found nowhere but
in Him, and He is the only "other" in which there is an existence of God
in the proper sense, so far, that is, as we posit the God-consciousness in
His self-consciousness as continually and exclusively determining every
moment, and consequently also this perfect indwelling of the Supreme
Being as His peculiar being and His inmost self. Indeed, working backwards we must now say, if it is only through Him that the human God-
consciousness becomes an existence of God in human nature, and only
through the rational nature that the totality of finite powers can become an
existence of God in the world, that in truth He alone mediates all existence
of God in the world and all revelation of God through the world, in so far
as He bears within Himself the whole new creation which contains and
develops the potency of the God-consciousness.

*Kathryn Tanner, "Jesus Christ," in* The Cambridge Companion
to Christian Doctrine, *ed. Colin E. Gunton (Cambridge:*
*Cambridge University Press, 1997), 258, 260–61*

For Schleiermacher, historical investigation is not the appropriate means
to arrive at beliefs about Jesus Christ the Redeemer; everything that a
theologian needs to know about Jesus can be derived from the nature of
Christian piety itself. For Bultmann, only the Christ proclaimed in the
New Testament and subsequent Christian witness has importance for theology; historical investigation into the life and death of Jesus, aside from
merely confirming the historical fact that he existed, has no place in
grounding, validating or adjudicating Christian faith claims. Rather than
raising epistemological questions about Christian belief's genesis from or

logical dependence on historical investigation, the Jesus of history/Christ of faith problematic represents in their work a way of talking about a variety of closely related christological topics. Thus, the two terms "Jesus of history" and "Christ of faith" are used, respectively, to talk about the relation between Jesus and his effects on those he saves (Schleiermacher), or to talk about the relation between Jesus Christ and the Holy Spirit poured out among us (Bultmann). The two terms also stand in for the humiliation of Jesus, on the one hand, and his exaltation, on the other (the earthly Jesus of the crucifixion and the risen Lord). . . .

The results are problematic for dogmatics. In Schleiermacher's case, where Jesus of history/Christ of faith becomes the modern translation of Christian talk about the relation between Jesus and his saving effects, the inability to distinguish adequately between the terms means that the divinity of Jesus and the human nature of those he affects are blurred. The divine dimension of Jesus' life must mimic (albeit in a perfect form) the character of Christian piety as an experience of him. Jesus has to have in his own right that superiority of God-consciousness which arises in Christian consciousness of him.

The persons of the Trinity, which were distinct in previous theological discussion of the order of reality, also tend now to blur. The Word of Jesus Christ seems impossible to distinguish from the faith that is poured out by the Holy Spirit for the community of Christians; the Word of Jesus Christ seems submerged or dissolved within it. Therefore Bultmann can say that the proclamation of Christians "has put itself in the place of the historical Jesus; it represents him". It "has, as it were, displaced [him]." . . .

It may be that, contrary to the impression of submergence, the kerygma, or Christian proclamation of the saving significance of Jesus Christ, is salvific here for the very reason that Jesus is present in it; the kerygma saves by making the saving events of the cross present now. But it is still the case that the salvific power of Jesus seems strangely confined to Christian faith and proclamation, the two being closely associated in traditional terms with the Holy Spirit. The cross of Jesus seems to have no saving power in itself; it would be an insignificant fact of past history apart from them.

## 2.2 The Quest for the Historical Jesus

*Bultmann and Tillich are typical responses to the failure of the first quest for the historical Jesus that began with Reimarus at the end of the eighteenth century and lasted until Albert Schweitzer established its essentially flawed character (in*

The Quest of the Historical Jesus, *ET 1910) as simply a backward projection of the writers' own values. Beginning in the 1950s, however, Bultmann's famous pupil Ernst Käsemann inaugurated a new quest, which the following extract from Schillebeeckx reflects.*

*Edward Schillebeeckx*, Jesus, *trans. Hubert Hoskins*
*(London: Collins; New York: Seabury Press, 1979), 71–72*

As over against R. Bultmann, who is by no means sceptical about the possibility of a systematic and historical reconstruction of "Jesus of Nazareth" but denies the theological relevance of such an enterprise, post-Bultmann exegesis, especially since E. Käsemann, has been right to relativize the distinction between "Jesus of Nazareth" and the "Christ of the Church". This trend has become fairly general. The older *Formgeschichte* [*the study of how the form in which Jesus' sayings were presented reflects the church's concerns of the time*] looked for the seedbed of the Jesus-tradition solely in the Christian community after Jesus' death, which entailed its putting the main emphasis on the discontinuity between Jesus as a historical figure and the Christ proclaimed by the Church. In recent years, however, exegesis has tended more and more to make room for the social intercourse and fellowship of (the) disciples with Jesus during his earthly life. Within the total picture of the biblical Jesus Christ, therefore, the continuity between the historical Jesus and the "Christ proclaimed" is starting to come into focus more than it had done before, even though opinion as to its concrete form is still sharply divided. This new set of bearings, as it were, have served to show that the New Testament was indeed written in the context of the Church's professed belief that Jesus is the crucified-and-risen One, but that people were also very much aware of the historical tension between the Christian experience of the exalted Christ present in the believing community and the recollection of the life Jesus had lived on earth. The biblical text contains all kinds of signals pointing to that awareness. On that basis it is possible up to a point—quite adequately, at any rate—to mark off what was being recollected of Jesus' life on earth from the process of overlaying it, which stems from the situation obtaining in the primitive Church. And even where this turns out to be in substance impossible, it remains true that for the very sake of the Christian *kerygma* a "historical" concern with Jesus forms part of the source of the tradition, the deposit of which was found in and even prior to the synoptic gospels. The likely assumption is, therefore, that the Jesus whom the gospels present resembles—not of course in every detail but substantially—the historically "real thing", in spite of all the Church's updating activities. Thus modern exegesis has abandoned Bultmann's principle that "the preaching of Jesus belongs to the premises of the theology of the New Testament and forms no part of that theology as such". The rather abrupt discontinuity which *kerygma* theologians had postulated between the proclaiming Jesus and the Christ proclaimed is being very much relativized at the moment. It is not denied that the four gospels are extensively conditioned by the confessional affirmation, proclamation, catechesis, paraenesis and liturgy of the first Christian congregations, and so are overlaid with the evangelists' own theology; but they are thought none the less to contain sufficient basic information about Jesus and recollections of him, in respect of his message, his attitude to life and his conduct as a whole.

N. T. *Wright,* Jesus and the Victory of God
*(London: SPCK, 1996), 84–86, 651–53*

*More recently, a "third quest" has been identified in writers such as John Dominic Crossan, E. P. Sanders, Gerd Thiessen, and Geza Vermes. Its chief characteristic is its primary focus on Jesus' contemporary context in the Judaism of the time. While someone like N. T. Wright is confident of secure results, great divergences remain among its practitioners.*

First, some general remarks about the Third Quest. There is now a real attempt to do history seriously. Josephus, so long inexplicably ignored is suddenly and happily in vogue. There is a real willingness to be guided by first-century sources, and to see the Judaism of that period in all its complex pluriformity, with the help now available from modern studies of the history and literature of the period. Qumran and the apocalyptic writings are not merely part of the dark backcloth against which the great light of the gospel shines the more brightly; they are part of the historical evidence for the world of first-century Palestine. Certain basic questions emerge: Jesus' message is evaluated, not for its timeless significance, but for the meaning it must have had for the audience of his own day, who had their minds full of poverty and politics, and would have had little time for theological abstractions or timeless verities. The crucifixion, long recognized as an absolute bedrock in history, is now regularly made the centre of understanding: what must Jesus have been like if he ended up on a Roman cross? . . .

If we start with historical questions such as these, there are important consequences for our method. We do not need to detach Jesus' sayings from the rest of the evidence, and examine them in isolation. . . . This is

the burden of Sanders' section on method, and I think he is right. . . . Bultmann was determined that, though Jesus was historically a first-century
Jew, his first-century Jewishness was precisely not the place where his "significance" lay. The renewed "New Quest", following this line, has often
played down the specifically Jewish features of Jesus, stressing instead
those which he may have shared with other Mediterranean cultures; it has
also downplayed to a large extent the significance of Jesus' death, stressing that we know very little about it and suggesting that the earliest Christians were not particularly interested in it—a feature, of course, which
marks a break with Bultmann himself. The present "Third Quest", by and
large, will have none of this. Jesus must be understood as a comprehensible and yet, so to speak, crucifiable first-century Jew, whatever the theological or hermeneutical consequences. . . .

I have argued that Jesus' underlying aim was based on his faith-
awareness of vocation. He believed himself called, by Israel's god, to *evoke*
the traditions which promised YHWH's return to Zion, and the somewhat more nebulous but still important traditions which spoke of a human
figure sharing the divine throne; to *enact* those traditions in his own journey to Jerusalem, his messianic act in the Temple, and his death at the
hands of the pagans (in the hope of subsequent vindication); and thereby
to *embody* YHWH's return. His intentions, putting those aims into practice, involved the detail of the journey, of his arrival in Jerusalem and
action in the Temple, of the Last Supper, of his agonizing wait in the gar-
den, and of his refusal to offer any defence of himself before the authorities. He carried out those intentions, believing that he was thereby
accomplishing those aims.

Jesus' beliefs, therefore, remained those of a first-century Jew, committed to the coming kingdom of Israel's god. He did not waver in his loyalty
to Jewish doctrine. But his beliefs were those of a first-century Jew *who
believed that the kingdom was coming in and through his own work.* His loyalty
to Israel's cherished beliefs therefore took the form of critique and renova-
tion from within; of challenge to traditions and institutions whose true purpose, he believed (like prophets long before, and radicals in his own day),
had been grievously corrupted and distorted; and of new proposals which,
though without precedent, were never mere innovation. They always
claimed the high ground: fulfilment, completion, consummation. . . .

I suggest, in short, that the return of YHWH to Zion, and the Temple-
theology which it brings into focus, are the deepest keys and clues to
gospel christology. Forget the "titles" of Jesus, at least for a moment; forget the pseudo-orthodox attempts to make Jesus of Nazareth conscious of

being the second person of the Trinity; forget the arid reductionism that is the mirror-image of that unthinking would-be orthodoxy. Focus, instead, on a young Jewish prophet telling a story about YHWH returning to Zion as judge and redeemer, and then embodying it by riding into the city in tears, symbolizing the Temple's destruction and celebrating the final exodus. I propose, as a matter of history, that Jesus of Nazareth was conscious of a vocation: a vocation, given him by the one he knew as "father", to enact in himself what, in Israel's scriptures, God had promised to accomplish all by himself. He would be the pillar of cloud and fire for the people of the new exodus. He would embody in himself the returning and redeeming action of the covenant God.

## 2.3 The Watershed of the Resurrection

*Gerald O'Collins, SJ*, The Easter Jesus
*(London: Darton, Longman & Todd, 1980), 59–61*

We risk turning the historian into a theologian, if we ask him to include the resurrection among the proper objects of his study. He deals normally with events that have human and other natural causes. We ought to have serious misgivings about requiring an historian to recognise and integrate into his explanations alleged "special" interventions *in history*, whether merely providential or miraculous. At most he may be expected to record and offer some elucidation of the fact that the Babylonian captivity, the fall of Jerusalem in AD 70 and other biblical events were acknowledged by certain people as "acts of God". It is not the historian's duty to verify (or refute?) the claim that God "deeply" engaged himself in these events and so disclosed in a special way his intentions. The resurrection lies much more outside the proper sphere of historical studies, and that for two reasons. The New Testament both (1) expounds this event as the transit of the dead Jesus *out of history* to a glorified life in the "other" world of God, and (2) attributes it to divine causality *alone*. Unlike the fall of Jerusalem where Titus and the Roman soldiers played their role, the resurrection was *ex hypothesi* effected only by God. . . .

Nevertheless, it would be wrong to repudiate all involvement of the historian in our assessment of Christ's resurrection. The allegation that women discovered the tomb to be empty obviously remains open to ordinary historical investigation. Likewise, the historian can examine the testimony of that particular group of men who claimed Easter appearances at a particular time in a particular country. He may discuss the possibility of their being hallucinated at the time, as well as the results of this experience in their later lives. He can dispose of theories about their having created the whole story on the basis of some myth about a dying and rising God.

Finally, the historian can mark off the alleged resurrection in terms of ordinary time. Granted that the actual resurrection was a creative action of God on the crucified and buried Jesus of Nazareth, nevertheless, it was alleged to have happened at a particular time. At one time men did not say, "God has raised Jesus from the dead". At a subsequent time they said just that. There exists an historical "fringe" to the resurrection which calls for the historian's attention, even if he rightly refuses to take the event itself as an object for his direct study.

By speaking of "fringe" questions, I do not wish to rule out *a priori* the possibility that the historian could disprove the resurrection. Given appropriate evidence, he might establish that the women visited the wrong grave, that grave-robbers stole the body, that the apostles perpetrated a deliberate fraud, or even that Jesus was not executed under Pontius Pilate at all. Without the crucifixion there would have been no resurrection. While the resurrection may not be open to positive proof by the historian, he could in principle demonstrate that certain presuppositions (for example, that Jesus lived and died) or attendant claims (for example, that his grave was discovered to be empty) were false. In brief, if the historian cannot verify the resurrection, he could in principle disprove it.

Hence it is not open to us to claim that the resurrection has nothing at all to do with historical enquiry. Easter faith does not prove totally immune to historical judgements, as if it belonged to a special, religious sphere.

*Hans Küng,* On Being a Christian, *trans. Edward Quinn*
*(London: Collins, 1977), 357–60*

The Crucified *lives.* What does "lives" mean here? What is concealed behind the diverse time-conditioned ideal types and narrative forms which the New Testament uses to describe it? . . .

*No return to this life in space and time.* . . . Jesus' resurrection must not be confused with the raisings of the dead scattered about in the ancient literature of miracle workers (even confirmed with doctors' attestations) and reported in three instances of Jesus (daughter of Jairus, young man of Nain, Lazarus). Quite apart from the historical credibility of such legendary accounts (Mark, for instance, has nothing about the sensational raising of Lazarus from the dead), what is meant by the raising of Jesus is just not the revival of a corpse. Even in Luke's account Jesus did not simply return to biological-earthly life, in order—like those raised from the dead—to die again. No, according to the New Testament conception, he has the final frontier of death definitively behind him. He has entered into a wholly different, imperishable, eternal, "heavenly" life: into the life of God, for which—as we have seen—very diverse formulas and ideas were used in the New Testament.

*Not a continuation of this life in space and time.* Even to speak of life "after" death is misleading: eternity is not characterized by "before" and "after". It means a new life which escapes the dimensions of space and time, a life within God's invisible imperishable, incomprehensible domain. It is not simply an endless "further": "further life," "carrying on further," "going on further." But it is something definitively "new": new creation, new birth, new man and new world. That which finally breaks through the return of the eternal sameness of "dying and coming to be." What is meant is to be definitively with God and so to have definitive life.

*Assumption into ultimate reality.* If we are not to talk in metaphors, raising (resurrection) and exaltation (taking up, ascension, glorification) must be seen as one identical, single happening. And indeed as a happening in connection with death in the impenetrable hiddenness of God. The Easter message in all its different variations means simply one thing: Jesus did not die into nothingness. In death and from death he *died into and was taken up* by that *incomprehensible and comprehensive ultimate reality* which we designate by the name of *God.* When man reaches his eschaton, the absolutely final point in his life, what awaits him? Not nothing, as even believers in nirvana would say. But that All which for Jews, Christians and Muslims is God. Death is transition to God, is retreat into God's hiddenness, is assumption into his glory. Strictly speaking, only an atheist can say that death is the *end of everything.* . . .

Do we need then expressly to insist on the fact that man's new life, involving as it does the ultimate reality, God himself, is *a priori* a matter of *faith*? It is an event of the new creation, which breaks through death as the last frontier and therefore the horizon of our world and thought as a whole. For it means the definitive breakthrough of one dimensional man into the truly other dimension: the evident reality of God and the rule of the Crucified, calling men to follow him. Nothing is easier than to raise doubts about this. Certainly "pure reason" is faced here with an impassable frontier. At this point we can only agree with Kant. Nor can the resurrection be proved by historical arguments; traditional apologetics breaks down here. Since man is here dealing with God and this by definition means with the invisible, impalpable, uncontrollable, only one attitude is appropriate and required: believing trust, trusting faith. There is no way to the risen Christ and to eternal life which bypasses faith. The resurrection is not a miracle authenticating faith. It is itself the object of faith.

*Karl Barth*, Dogmatics in Outline, *trans. G. T. Thomson (London: SCM Press, 2001), 112–14*

Man is no longer seriously regarded by God as a sinner. Whatever he may be, whatever there is to be said of him, whatever he has to reproach himself with, God no longer takes him seriously as a sinner. He has died to sin; there on the Cross of Golgotha. He is no longer present for sin. He is acknowledged before God and established as a righteous man, as one who does right before God. As he now stands, he has, of course, his existence in sin and so in its guilt; but he has that behind him. The turn has been achieved, once for all. But we cannot say, "I have turned away once for all, I have experienced"—no; "once for all" is Jesus Christ's "once for all". But if we believe in Him, then it holds for us. Man is in Christ Jesus, who has died for him, in virtue of His Resurrection, God's dear child, who may live by and for the good pleasure of God.

If that is the message of Easter, then you realise that in the Resurrection of Jesus Christ there is the revelation of the still hidden fruit of Christ's death. It is this very turning-point which is still hidden in the death of Christ, hidden under the aspect in which man there appears consumed by the wrath of God. And now the New Testament bears us witness, that this aspect of man is not the meaning of the event upon Golgotha, but that behind this aspect the real meaning of this event is the one which is revealed on the third day. On this third day there begins a new story of man, so that we may even divide the life of Jesus into two great periods, the thirty-three years to His death, and the quite short and decisive period of the forty days between His death and the Ascension. The third day a new life of Jesus begins; but at the same time on the third day there begins a new *Aeon*, a new shape of the world, after the old world has been completely done away and settled in the death of Jesus Christ. Easter is the breaking in of a new time and world in the existence of the man Jesus, who now begins a new life as the conqueror, as the victorious bearer, as the destroyer of the burden of man's sin, which had been laid upon Him. In this altered existence of His the first community saw not only a supernatural continuation of His previous life, but an entirely new life, that of the exalted Jesus Christ, and simultaneously the beginning of a new *world*. . . .

The Resurrection of Jesus Christ reveals, it completes this proclamation of victory. We must not transmute the Resurrection into a spiritual event. We must listen to it and let it tell us the story how there was an empty grave, that new life beyond death did become visible.

*Allan D. Galloway*, Wolfhart Pannenberg
*(London: George Allen & Unwin, 1973)*, 77–80

Many attempts have been made in the past to trace the doctrine of the divinity of the Christ back to the earthly life of Jesus. This has been difficult in view of the known tendency of the early church to read its own theology back into the pre-Easter life and teaching of Jesus and to put its own theology into his mouth. This means that every claim to divine status ascribed to Jesus must be suspect. Moreover, it is difficult to reconcile such an open claim with true human consciousness.

In view of such difficulties, others like Bultmann have attempted to find the source of the doctrine of the person of Christ in the faith of the early church. . . .

Pannenberg's suggestion that the belief in the divinity of Christ is to be traced directly to the resurrection is more plausible than either of these. It adequately explains the rise of the belief in the divinity of Jesus and why that belief should have coloured so heavily the reporting of his earthly life. It has the added attraction that it leaves open the possibility that Jesus had (in this particular sense) divine status and yet in his earthly life experienced the limitations essential to human consciousness. If this position can stand critical examination, then it solves many of the perennial problems and contradictions of christology.

Pannenberg's argument (as is so often the case) looks speciously simple. In fact it is both complex and subtle. . . . God cannot be fully disclosed in history until the end of history, for the future is always open and further radical novelty is always possible. Apocalyptic arrives at the notion of the totality and the completion of history. In that completion or end of history, the Glory of God will be fully revealed. That end or completion of history includes the general resurrection of the dead. This is the only context in which Jewish tradition considers resurrection. Therefore when Jesus rises from the dead there is no option but to treat this event as a foretaste of the end. Therefore the self-disclosure of God is complete in Jesus Christ, risen and glorified.

But where self-disclosure is complete it must be a once-for-all event. Any further disclosure would imply the incompleteness of the former disclosure. Therefore the event must be unique.

Furthermore, where self-disclosure is complete there must be real identity of the person disclosed and the disclosing medium. Otherwise the medium would obscure the self-disclosure to some extent and the disclosure would not be complete. Therefore there must be a real identity of God and the risen Christ. Thus the doctrine of the incarnation derives from and is dependent on the recognition of Jesus as the final revelation of God. This derives from an acknowledgement of the reality of his resurrection as historic event and recognition of the meaning of that event within its apocalyptic context. This order of knowing cannot be reversed.

Granted for the moment then that this is the order of knowing (*ordo cognoscendi*), what of the order of being (*ordo essendi*)? That is to say, granted that it is in the resurrection that Jesus is *recognised* as the Christ who is one with God, is that also the moment in which he *becomes* the Christ of God? There are passages, especially in the earliest strata of the New Testament tradition, which might suggest an affirmative answer [*e.g., Rom. 1:3–4*]. . . .

Pannenberg is sympathetic to the symbol of adoption as it appears in the New Testament. "Nevertheless", he says:

> the idea that Jesus had received divinity only as a consequence of his resurrection is not tenable. We have seen in our discussion of the meaning of the resurrection event that the character of the confirmation of Jesus' pre-Easter claim is connected with the resurrection. To this extent the resurrection event has retroactive power. Jesus did not simply become something that he previously had not been, but his pre-Easter claim was confirmed by God. This confirmation, the manifestation of Jesus' "divine Sonship" by God, is the new thing brought by the Easter event. However, as confirmation, the resurrection has retroactive force for Jesus' pre-Easter activity, which taken by itself was not yet recognisable as being divinely authorized and its authorization was also not yet definitively settled. However, this has been revealed in its divine legitimation in the light of Jesus' resurrection. (*Jesus—God and Man*, ET 1968, p. 135)

*Wolfhart Pannenberg*, Systematic Theology, *vol. 3,*
*trans. Geoffrey W. Bromiley (Grand Rapids: Wm. B. Eerdmans;*
*Edinburgh: T. & T. Clark, 1998), 604–5, 628–30*

In the duration of creaturely existence, the eternal self-identity of God finds only a remote and more or less broken echo, especially in our case. Only in the history of Jesus of Nazareth did the eschatological future, and with it the eternity of God, really enter the historical present. This is what the church's confession of the incarnation of the Son in the person of Jesus tells us. Precisely by his self-distinction from the Father in his preaching and conduct Jesus showed himself . . . to be the Son of the eternal Father, and the future of the kingdom that he proclaimed as coming became the present already in what he said and did.

The inbreaking of the present of the coming kingdom is granted to others also insofar as they accept the message of Jesus and open themselves to his work. Thus he said that if he by the finger of God cast out demons, then the kingdom of God had already come to them (Luke 11:20). The Johannine Christ says the same thing relative to the eschatological future of the resurrection and the judgment: Those who hear his word and believe in him who has sent him have eternal life and will not come into judgment, but have already passed from death into life (John 5:24). . . .

We find the same structure in Paul's well-known statements about the Already and the Not Yet of salvation. Already in the present believers by baptism are buried with Christ in his death (Rom. 6:3), and they are thus free of sin (v. 7) and reconciled to God even though on their earthly path death is still ahead of them. They have a share already in the Spirit of the new life (8:11) even though their resurrection is still future (cf. 6:5). Like John, Colossians is bold enough to describe the resurrection of the baptized as a reality that is present already (2:12), although here, too, the tension with the future of salvation is retained when it says that the new life of believers is still hidden with Christ in God, to whom he has been exalted (3:3–4).

The same tension even permeates christological statements, and that not merely in the backward glances of Easter faith to the relation of the earthly course of Jesus to the identity of the Son of God that became manifest in his resurrection and that retrospectively defines the identity of the pre-Easter person of Jesus. There is a similar tension in the relation of the present reality of the exalted Lord to the subjection of demonic powers that will come only with his return. Already at the right hand of the Father the risen Christ has been invested with lordship (Phil. 2:9–10), but on earth the battle still goes on (1:30), and only at Christ's return will it be concluded by the power with which he can subdue all things to himself (3:21). . . .

The crucified Lord experienced the resurrection from the dead as this individual in distinction from all others. Yet the new life imparted to him relates to that of a totality, a new humanity, for which he is the author of salvation (Heb. 2:10; Acts 3:15) and which is fashioned in his likeness (1 Cor. 15:49). According to 2 Cor. 3:18 this event means that we shall be changed into the image, not just a copy, of the risen Lord. In keeping is the Pauline thought that the body of the risen Lord is not just Jesus' individual form of existence but embraces his community as well. The community is linked to Christ in the unity of the *one* body, of *his* body (1 Cor. 12:27; Rom. 12:4–5). The root of this Pauline thought is to be sought in the eucharistic tradition. Expositors are usually too timid to follow through on this statement in all its boldness and to take it literally rather than as a figure of speech or as a statement about a "mystical" body that is different from Christ's resurrection body. But if we take what Paul says about the church as the body of Christ just as it stands, it follows that we must understand the new life of the resurrection, the life of the risen Christ, as a removal of the individual autonomy and separation that are part of the corporeality of earthly life, though with no simple erasure of individual particularity. This is primarily true of the corporeality of the risen Christ. If Jesus gave his life for the salvation of the world, the new life of the risen Lord, even as bodily life, cannot have a form of existence that separates it from others. If the resurrection appearances in the Gospel traditions involve only individual corporeality for the risen Lord, they betray a one-sidedness that needs correction by the Pauline concept of the church as the body of Christ. . . .

The distinction between head and body preserves the individual distinction of Jesus from his people notwithstanding his unity with them in the fellowship of his body. Similarly we must say of the resurrection of believers that their individuality will not disappear even though their separation from each other in their earthly existence is one of the things that will be profoundly changed by the eschatological transformation of this mortal life into the new corporeality of the resurrection from the dead. Individuals become members of *one* body when they no longer have to assert themselves against one another, but mutually accept one another for what they are in their individuality, and for what in this way they are also *for others*, just as they accept the Father in his deity and Jesus Christ as their Head and Lord. In all these relations not only particularity but also its positive acceptance, and therefore also self-distinction, are still the condition of fellowship, the same being true in relation to God. Yet now distinction no longer means separation because individuals are no longer seeking to "be as God" but living out their own finitude in its relation to the individuality of others. There is thus disclosed the deeper basis of the connection between the revelation of the glory of Christ and the glorifying of those who are related to him by faith at his coming again, including the transforming of the world itself into a new heaven and a new earth.

The expectation of Christ's return is not oriented to the appearing of a single individual but to the making manifest of a vital nexus originating in the crucified Jesus of Nazareth in the light of the glory of God.

## Topics for Discussion

1. Is faith in Christ a response to the actual life, death, and resurrection of Jesus, or is it a response to what he taught (or perhaps to what the church believed he taught)? What differences might each of these answers make?
2. Does history always assume some particular point of view? Is an "objective" or "scientific" history impossible? How do these questions impact on the study of the person of Jesus?
3. How important is Jesus' Jewish context for understanding his message and significance?
4. To what extent does it make sense to speak of the resurrection as an objective event? Is there something more to the religious content of the resurrection than the message of the cross?
5. How does Christ's resurrection affect the life of the believer? Does it say something about the cross and our vindication, or about the future coming of the kingdom of God, or what?

*Chapter Three*

# The Human God?

## 3.1 Classical Two-Natures Christology: The Divine Working through the Human

*Athanasius*, De Incarnatione, *18–19*
*(trans. Robert W. Thomson, in* Athanasius: Contra Gentes
and De Incarnatione *[Oxford: Clarendon Press, 1971], 177–79, 181)*

18. When therefore the theologians who speak of him say that he ate and drank and was born, know that the body was born as a body and was nourished on suitable food; but God the Word, who was with the body yet orders the universe, also made known through his actions in the body that he himself was not a man but God the Word. But these things are said of him, because the body which ate and was born and suffered was no one else's but the Lord's; and since he became man, it was right for these things to be said of him as a man, that he might be shown to have a true, not an unreal, body. But as thereby he was known to be bodily present, so by the works which he did through the body he proved himself to be the Son of God. So he cried to the unbelieving Jews and said: "*If I do not do the works of my Father, do not believe me; but if I do do them, even if you do not believe in me, believe in my works, that you may know and realise that the Father is in me and I am in the Father*" [John 10:37–38]. For as he is invisible yet is known by the works of creation, so, becoming a man and not visible in a body, it would have been known from his works that it was not a man but the Power of God and Word who was performing them. For the fact that he commanded demons and cast them out was not a human deed, but a divine one. Or who, seeing him healing the diseases to which the race of men

was subject, would still think that he was a man and not God? For he puri-
fied lepers, he made the lame to walk, he opened the hearing of the deaf,
he made the blind to see, and indeed cast out every illness and disease from
men; from which anyone could see his divinity. For who, having seen him
giving what was lacking to those whose very being was deficient and open-
ing the eyes of the man blind from birth, would not think that the creating of men was in his power and that he was their Fashioner and Maker?
For he who gave to a man what was missing from birth is most clearly the
Lord of the creation of men. Therefore also in the beginning, when he
came down to us, he fashioned for himself the body from a virgin, in order
to give all men no small indication of his divinity; for he who fashioned
this is himself the Maker of these others. For who, seeing that the body
came forth from a virgin alone without a man, would not think that he
who was revealed in it was the Creator and Lord of the other bodies? And
who, seeing the substance of water being changed and turned into wine,
would not think that he who did this was Lord and Creator of the substance of all water? . . .

19. It seemed good to our Saviour to do all these things in order that,
since men had not recognized his providence in the universe nor had they
understood his divinity from his creation, if they looked up on account of
the works of the body, they might gain through him an idea of the knowledge of the Father, working to an understanding of his universal providence from its individual aspects, as I said above. For who, seeing his
power over demons, or who, seeing the demons confess that he is their
Lord, would still be doubtful in his mind whether he is the Son and Wisdom and Power of God? Nor did he cause creation itself to be silent, but,
what is most amazing, even at his death—or rather at the victory over
death, I mean the cross—the whole of creation was confessing that he who
was known and suffered in the body was not simply a man, but the Son of
God and Saviour of all. For the sun turned back, and the earth shook, and
the mountains were rent, and all were terrified; and these things showed
that Christ who was on the cross was God, and that the whole of creation
was his handmaid and was witnessing in fear to the coming of her master.
So in this way God the Word revealed himself to men through his works.

*Willie James Jennings, "He Became Truly Human,"*
Modern Theology *12 (1996): 244–48*

"He became truly human." These stunning words of the Nicene Creed
need again to have an educative function among Christians. . . . We need

again to assert these words as the basis for knowing what it means to be human. . . .

However, if the "One Lord Jesus Christ who became truly human" is the key to knowing our humanity, then we need again to take crucial theological advice from two early church figures. From Irenaeus, Bishop of Lyons we need to remember how it is that we as Christians are to map out the meaning of the material, the meaning of real humanity. And from Athanasius, Bishop of Alexandria we need to relearn the difference between affirming authentic flesh and denying the false flesh. . . .

For Irenaeus, the created world, its redemption in Christ, and its future hopes are all tied inseparably together. *For Irenaeus, there is no emancipation without incarnation*. Without the One become flesh, there is no hope in the flesh. Yet there is hope and joy in the flesh for us all because the One who redeems is the one who has created. Thus we can trust, we can believe and live in the world, no longer distrusting form nor fearful of the fragility of the material. Irenaeus gives us a theological map that runs from the body of Jesus to the creation to its final consummation, picking up tradition and scripture on the way. From Irenaeus we learn that whenever the desire for emancipation is separated from the reality of the incarnation, Jesus' body becomes merely a fleeting liberating *form* while the desire for freedom becomes primary and eternal. Yet Irenaeus' was no simple and straightforward victory over Gnostic forces. [*Gnosticism saw the body as unimportant, or sometimes even as evil.*] His invocation of a "rule of faith" in part was to help establish a *line of flesh* that can be trusted going all the way back to the body of Jesus. . . .

Between Irenaeus of Lyons and Athanasius of Alexandria lies not merely the time of centuries and the distance between Asia Minor [*where Irenaeus had been born*] and Alexandria, but the development of a new, more sophisticated distrust of human flesh. . . .

This world of fourth century Christianity understood the profound difference between the ruler and those who were ruled, the difference between the One who is to be obeyed and the ones who obey. To forget this difference is to place yourself, indeed all of society, at the door of chaos. Order, justice, and freedom are assured as long as we do not confuse the order of power—there is the great ruler and those in subjection. There is the creator and the creature, and the two must never be confused. Athanasius understood this difference, and so did another older, more established and charismatic . . . Arius. For Arius, Jesus the Christ was a creature just like us, only differing in his quality and quantity of obedience to God. Arius (and those who were to follow his line of thinking) would not allow the creator into this world. God is perfect, uncreated, and pure, and even at our best, we are yet fallible, weak, impure creatures. Jesus, for Arius, was indeed the best we will ever become, the proto-type for us, created creator, but he was still only us. He revealed *our possibilities* under the rulership of the sovereign God. He holds out before us what we can do, if we persevere to the end. Arianism never denied God, it denied the real embodiment of God in creaturely flesh. Humanity only points the way to God; it cannot be God.

Athanasius understood that if the incarnate One was not the very flesh of God found in the contingencies and weaknesses of real human life, then our salvation was not real, but only a real *possibility*—only what *could be* if we engaged in the right *praxis*, even the *praxis* of obedience. The difference between Athanasius and Arius comes down to the difference between a humanity saved and liberated by the actual hands of God and thus joined together in the body of Jesus [and a] humanity that is yet to be liberated by the work of its own hands and is thus joined together only by the *needed work* of liberation itself. In this latter vision, then, Jesus has great value because he shows where *our* work must be engaged; he becomes the marker of the places of needed emancipation.

Yet for Athanasius, this represents the false flesh of Christ that we must deny in light of affirming the full divinity of Jesus. Only in the context of this affirmation can we see our authentic humanity, and engage in authentic liberation. . . .

Athanasius refused to break the incarnation in half, with one half being the presentation of the likeness of God among us (i.e. *homoiousios*) and another half being the presentation of the actions God calls us to do (i.e. divinity by obedience). From this great bishop we must relearn that if *God* is "spared from" the trouble of being human, then we will experience *no* salvation, but only the often suffocating negotiation between which images properly present God and which actions are appropriately called for by God. Together Irenaeus and Athanasius point to a crucial reality for us: we must trust human flesh as the bearer of the divine life.

### 3.2 Incarnation as Kenosis: The Self-Emptying of Divinity

*Cyril of Alexandria, Third Letter to Nestorius (430)*
*(trans. Lionel R. Wickham, in* Cyril of Alexandria: Select Letters
*[Oxford: Clarendon Press, 1983], 17)*

We declare that the flesh was not changed into the nature of Godhead and that neither was the inexpressible nature of God the Word converted into the nature of flesh. He is, indeed, utterly unchangeable and immutable ever remaining, as the Bible says, the same; even when a baby seen in swaddling clothes at the bosom of the Virgin who bore him, he still filled the whole creation as God and was co-regent with his sire—for deity is measureless, sizeless and admits of no bounds.

*John Calvin*, Institutes of the Christian Religion *2.14.3,*
*ed. John T. McNeill, trans. Ford Lewis Battles*
*(Philadelphia: Westminster Press; London: SCM Press, 1960), 485–86*

"Christ will deliver the Kingdom to his God and Father" [1 Cor. 15:24]. Surely the Kingdom of the Son of God had no beginning and will have no end. But even as he lay concealed under the lowness of flesh and "emptied himself, taking the form of a servant" [Phil. 2:7], laying aside the splendor of majesty, he showed himself obedient to his father [cf. Phil. 2:8]. Having completed this subjection, "he was at last crowned with glory and honor" [Heb. 2:9], and exalted to the highest lordship that before him "every knee should bow" [Phil. 2:10]. So then will he yield to the Father his name and crown of glory, and whatever he has received from the Father, that "God may be all in all" [1 Cor. 15:28]. For what purpose were power and lordship given to Christ, unless that by his hand the Father might govern us? In this sense, also, Christ is said to be seated at the right hand of the Father [cf. Mark 16:19; Rom. 8:34]. Yet this is but for a time, until we enjoy the direct vision of the Godhead. Here we cannot excuse the error of the ancient writers who pay no attention to the person of the Mediator, obscure the real meaning of almost all the teaching one reads in the Gospel of John, and entangle themselves in many snares. Let this, then, be our key to right understanding: those things which apply to the office of the Mediator are not spoken simply either of the divine nature or of the human. Until he comes forth as judge of the world Christ will therefore reign, joining us to the Father as the measure of our weakness permits. But when as partakers in heavenly glory we shall see God as he is, Christ, having then discharged the office of Mediator, will cease to be the ambassador of his Father, and will be satisfied with that glory which he enjoyed before the creation of the world. . . .

    . . . Then he returns the lordship to his Father so that—far from diminishing his own majesty—it may shine all the more brightly. Then, also, God shall cease to be the Head of Christ, for Christ's own deity will shine of itself, although as yet it is covered by a veil.

*P. T. Forsyth*, The Person and Place of Jesus Christ
*(London: Independent Press, 1909), 293–95, 296, 306–8*

If there was a personal pre-existence in the case of Christ it does not seem possible to adjust it to the historic Jesus without some doctrine of Kenosis. We face in Christ a Godhead self-reduced but real, whose infinite power took effect in self-humiliation, whose strength was perfected in weakness, who consented not to know with an ignorance divinely wise, and who emptied himself in virtue of his divine fulness. The alternative to a Kenosis used to be a Krypsis, or conscious concealment of the active divine glory for practical or strategic purposes. But that is now an impossible idea. While on the other hand an acquired Godhead would really be none. It would be but deification. And at bottom it is a contradiction. No creature could become God. . . .

We cannot form any scientific conception of the precise process by which a complete and eternal being could enter on a process of becoming, how Godhead could accept growth, how a divine consciousness could reduce its own consciousness by volition. If we knew and could follow that secret we should be God and not man. It is a difficulty partly ethical, partly psychological. Even if we admit psychologically that certain attributes could be laid aside—the less ethical attributes like omniscience, omnipotence, or ubiquity—could self-consciousness be thus impaired and a love still remain which was fully divine? And how can an infinite consciousness be thought of as reducing itself to a finite? God's infinite consciousness might indeed determine itself so as to pervade, sustain, and bind a variety of finite detail without losing consciousness. An immanent God, we believe, does so in creation. But if He parted with His self-consciousness as infinite would it not come as near to suicide as infinite could? . . .

. . . The suicide of God is no part of the kenotic idea, which turns but on self-divestment as a moral power of the eternal Son; who retains his consciousness but renounces the conditions of infinity and its precreate form. . . .

Most theories which attempt to deal with the Kenosis have set themselves to answer the question, What did the Son renounce in becoming man? What attributes of Godhead had to be surrendered for incarnation? And the replies have been various. Some have begun by a distinction between the relative and the immanent attributes of God. They have said that the relative attributes are those that were set up with the creation of a world, such as omnipotence, omniscience, and the like, which would have no meaning before a discrete creation was there; while the immanent attributes are those ethical and spiritual qualities, such as absolute love or holiness, without which God would not be God at all. And such thinkers have gone on to say that the Kenosis meant the renunciation of the former and the retention of the latter. Godhead in Christ parted with omniscience, and omnipotence, as with omnipresence; but it did not, and could not, part with absolute holiness or infinite love. Other theories have gone farther, and have seen in the Kenosis a renunciation of even such immanent attributes as a divine self-consciousness and absolute will.

In regard to the former class of theories the criticism is that even the relative attributes could not be parted with entirely. At most they must be thought of as latent and potential even were no created world there. They were ready when creation arose. They are equally necessary to Godhead with the immanent qualities which, again, cannot be wholly immanent, but must have a real relation to any world created by the Will of the absolute love.

In regard to the second class of theories, if the renunciation is carried so far as to part with a divine self-consciousness and will, it is not clear what is left in the way of identity or continuity at all. What is there, then, in common between the Eternal Son and the man Jesus? What remains of the divine nature when we extinguish the immanent ethical and personal qualities in any absolute sense?

To get over those difficulties we may perhaps take a happier course. Let us cease speaking of a nature as if it were an entity; of two natures as two independent entities; and let us think and speak of two modes of being, like quantitative and qualitative, or physical and moral. Instead of speaking of certain attributes as renounced may we not speak of a new mode of their being? The Son, by an act of love's omnipotence, set aside the style of a God, and took the style of a servant, the mental manner of a man, and the mode of moral action that marks human nature. (For morality, holiness, is surely not confined to the infinite mode alone.) He took the manner that marks a humanity not illustrious, not exceptional, but sheer and pure, where pomp has taken physic, and exposed itself to feel what wretches feel in life's awful storm. Take the attribute of omniscience, for instance. In its eternal form, it is an intuitive and simultaneous knowledge of all things; but when the Eternal enters time it becomes a discursive and successive knowledge, with the power to know all things only potential, and enlarging to become actual under the moral conditions that govern human growth and the extension of human knowledge. Here we have not so much the renunciation of attributes, nor their conscious possession and concealment, as the retraction of their mode of being from actual to potential. The stress falls on the mode of existence of these qualities, and not on their presence or absence. . . .

The attributes of God, like omniscience, are not destroyed when they are reduced to a potentiality. They are only concentrated. The self-reduction, or self-retraction, of God might be a better phrase than the self-emptying.

*John Austin Baker,* The Foolishness of God
*(London: Darton, Longman & Todd, 1970), 309–12*

How can a single personal being exist at the same time both as God and as true Man? Surely the same person cannot . . . be simultaneously a genuine human being and aware of himself as the eternal God? But if he is not aware of himself as God, then his identity has been destroyed; he is no longer truly himself. Hence orthodoxy has tried to formulate the structure of Jesus Christ in various ways. It has conceived that two natures, the divine and the human, each complete in itself, were, so to speak, screwed together to make a single being. Since this implies only one centre of conscious identity, one person, and since, if God is to become Man, the person must be that of God himself, the human component comes to be thought of as "impersonal". The deity takes on not a human being, for that would be impossible, but "human nature", complete with mind, feelings, will, and body, but not organized as the vehicle of an independent human personality. Such a conception leaves unresolved, however, the problem how a being conscious of himself as divine could live a normal human life. Hence the necessity is felt, sooner or later, of some kind of *kenosis*, or emptying. The divine person lays aside all his divine attributes. His power and knowledge and inviolable holiness are, as it were suspended, to enable him to conform himself to the narrow limits of human existence. In the end, therefore, we are left with the strange combination of a human nature without any personal centre, and a divine person existing in temporary unconsciousness of or detachment from his divine nature.

Such a diagram is the more unsatisfactory to us today, because of our very concept of "person", which the ancient world did not possess. The idea of a person without his nature, or of human nature existing except in a human person, is to us a contradiction in terms. It would seem, therefore, that if faith in the Incarnation is to be made comprehensible to the present age— and, whatever some may say, a belief must be comprehensible, at least in the sense of using words in a way that is not self-contradictory—then it must be done by starting from the concept of person. That this concept is as yet far from clear even in the human sciences no candid observer will deny. Too often it is used by writers today in a merely emotive sense: "The dignity of the person", "the great thing is to be a *person*"—where emphasis takes the place of analysis, and the hope seems to be that if only the word is repeated frequently and intensely enough, light will eventually dawn. But this only implies . . . that we have to understand God's world before we can hope to understand God, even to the best of our no doubt very limited capacity.

To approach the question from both ends at once, however, is not necessarily a hopeless task; and it may be that something can be said from the angle of God's entry into human life as well. It makes some difference, in fact, if we put the proposition that God becomes Man the other way round, and say, that *when God chooses to exist within the terms of our environment a man is what he becomes.* Manhood, in short, is the only mode of being in which God can do justice under such conditions to what he is.

If we think of the matter in this way, then certain traditionally worrying problems turn out not to be real problems at all. Manhood, for example, implies limited knowledge and limited powers. Perhaps most significant of all, it makes it impossible to believe in one's own perfection. However good a man was, if he were truly sensitive to the facts of the human condition, he could never assert that he was sinless. He might *be* sinless; he would not be sure that he was. If God became truly Man, therefore we would not expect him to be infallible on all questions, we would not expect him to claim to be morally immaculate. And if we had good reason to think that God might have become Man, then we would also conclude that these characteristics were not indispensable to his expressing the essence of his nature. What would be indispensable is that sacrificial love in loyalty to the good which the nature of things declares to be God's supreme value, and without which indeed he cannot even be believed to exist. To put the matter in New Testament terms, belief in the Incarnation demands not the Christ of the Fourth Gospel (and to a lesser extent of the other three) but the Jesus of history.

The real metaphysical difficulty, in the view of the present writer, is not one of dissecting the structure of the incarnate God. He cannot be dissected; he is himself. But we find ourselves bewildered by the notion of a single person existing at once within the terms of the created order, and also being continuously present to that order as its Creator. It may well be, however, when we think how relative and fluid is the whole system of Space and Time, and how elusive of our grasp, that this in fact presents no obstacle at all. One thing, from the theological angle, is clear: we cannot invoke some conception such as the doctrine of the Trinity to answer this question. God is not a committee, one of whose members can be detached to serve for a time on a foreign posting. Even if we wish, as well we may, to think that something analogous to society and relationship exists within God, yet God himself must remain indivisible, and be wholly committed to all his acts.

Two misgivings which may arise, and which are more relevant to our situation, are these. First, if we think in this way of God becoming Man, is it not inconceivable that the Man whom he becomes could ever be subject as we are to temptation? But why should this be so? . . . Conflict and ambiguity are of the essence of the human condition. Moral purity is attained not by an enormous aggregate of "correct" decisions in independent cases; for many cases there is no single "right solution", though there may be a number which we can definitely say are wrong. What is vital is that within the area of possible good solutions a man should choose in accordance with the demands of sacrificial love; and the pressures upon him not to do this are part of the condition of being human. The sinless man is therefore no more free from temptation than any other. His obedience to the true law of human existence is not a static and indefectible quality but a fulfilment which has to be achieved through suffering over and over again.

Secondly . . . the Jesus of history was mistaken about the programme which God planned to follow. To many this would seem to rule out at once any chance that he might be God in Man. But why? It is not merely natural in human beings to be in error about the details of the future, it is inevitable. This feature of the human condition could be overcome only by investing Jesus with superhuman powers which might indeed have satisfied the tired old dreams of paganism but would utterly exclude any true incarnation of God. What has inspired knowledge of the future to do with the point on which all really depends—perfect loyalty to the Good in love?

*Don Cupitt, "The Christ of Christendom," in* The Myth of God Incarnate, *ed. John Hick (London: SCM Press, 1993), 137*

The idea of kenosis in bourgeois Christian thought is clearly socially-conditioned. In a class society, where the Christian tradition was carried by people of very high status and privilege, there was need for christological validation of the duty to "condescend to men of low estate". The change in the connotations of the word "condescension" since those days gives us a revealing glimpse of theology's cultural relativity, and von Balthasar makes clear the hopeless inappropriateness of the idea of kenosis today.

*Hans Urs von Balthasar, "Jesus, the Absolutely Singular," in* The von Balthasar Reader, *ed. Medard Kehl, SJ, and Werner Löser, SJ, trans. Robert J. Daly, SJ, and Fred Lawrence (Edinburgh: T. & T. Clark, 1982), 129–31*

How much modern exegesis needs contemporary and future dogmatic theology . . . may be illustrated in conclusion by an especially critical example, that of Jesus' horizon of consciousness. The horizon of a genuine human person—and Jesus was one—is necessarily finite. Now a rather large number of texts, however, show undeniably that Jesus expected the arrival of the kingdom of God and with it the end of the world in the very near future; "some of those standing here" will experience this event before their death. The device of shifting this "apocalyptic imminent expectation" away from Jesus and attributing it primarily to the primitive church just doesn't work. Every means has been tried in order to read into some texts the supposition within Jesus himself of an "interval" between his death and his second coming, without striking success, we think, since one is dealing there with late levels of tradition or interpretations or churchly adjustments (to explain the delay of the *parousia*). Was Jesus then mistaken and—what is almost worse—did he mislead the primitive church to its unequivocal imminent expectation? Many, and not just liberal exegetes, flatly concede this in view of the textual evidence. Can the dogmatic theologians be satisfied with such information, or must they not, from their understanding of Jesus as the authentic interpreter of God, provide interpretative assistance? And can the dogmatic theologian do this without putting a muzzle on the text?

How would it be if Jesus had been completely right for himself? The ultimate horizon (says the dogmatic theologian) out of which he speaks is not the general apocalyptic of his time but the tremendous mandate of his Father to accomplish the atonement of the whole world with God, to "be finished with" the world, to reach the end of the world. As John puts it, to take away the sins of the world. He does not have to know in advance how this will be possible; enough that "the hour" of the Father will come, which no one ("not even the Son") knows; enough that the "hour of darkness" will be, which however introduces the end, brings the solution: "God made him to be sin," "in order to have mercy on all," says Paul. It is judgement and salvation at once, and through Jesus' fate ("I must be baptized with a baptism . . ."). Once again, he doesn't have to know anything about the cross, nay, he *should not* in order to achieve full obedience, know anything precise about it; the exactly spoken prophecies of the passion could be *vaticinia ex eventu* [*that is, "prophecies" composed subsequent to an event, in the light of what has already happened*]. But something horrible for him is coming, through which he will attain the end of the world, that he knows. And now it is extraordinary that this horror that stands before him does not force him to any kind of apocalyptic haste; he can project an ethic for believing existence which is not an "interim ethic" for a short time that is left but sounds as if all time was available to live it. That too is an expression of his perfect obedience, that he lives in the presently given day and leaves worry for the morrow to his Father. The only thing that is important is that each day be filled to the brim with doing the will of his Father. To that end he presses on, and not ("apocalyptically") to the approaching "hour" of the Father—and of darkness. For his active work he had his program, Israel, but in many ways pagans are already coming into his sphere of activity. Israel had long since been open to the nations in one way or another. Within this earthly mandate takes place the call of the Twelve, helpers in the mission, representatives to and judges of the tribes of Israel. He does what is possible within his active mandate whose horizon remains confined by his absolute obedience to the Father. Jesus *is not allowed to*, and will not, anticipate; in John 17 he entrusts his own, for the time of the passion, to the protection of the Father. [The] Cross is [the] end of the world (Matthew depicts it quite explicitly in these terms); Easter is a new world beyond the timeless abyss.

*Stephen T. Davis and C. Stephen Evans, "Conclusion: The Promise of Kenosis,"*
*in* Exploring Kenotic Christology, *ed. C. Stephen Evans*
*(Oxford: Oxford University Press, 2006), 314–16, 319–21*

We are personally convinced that some sort of kenosis is inevitable for orthodox or Chalcedonian Christians who have fully grasped the implications of the Incarnation. That fact will emerge, we believe, almost as soon as any sort of description is given of the Logos's transition from an exclusively divine mode of being to an incarnate mode of being. . . .

In John 13:1–20, a kind of mini-kenosis is described. During supper with the disciples, Jesus "got up from the table, took off his outer robe, and tied a towel around himself. Then he poured water into a basin and began to wash the disciples' feet and to wipe them with the towel that was tied around him." . . .

This act on the part of Jesus doubtless has many levels of meaning. Jesus' washing of their feet was surely meant to be symbolic of his imminent death on the cross, at which point—so Christians believe—our sins were atoned for and we were made clean. But after the foot washing, Jesus supplied a second explanation: he was setting an example for the disciples. He said: "Do you know what I have done to you? You call me teacher and Lord—and you are right, for that is what I am. So if I, your Lord and Teacher, have washed your feet, you also ought to wash one another's feet. . . . Servants are not greater than their master, nor are messengers greater than the one who sent them. If you know these things, you are blessed if you do them."

We call this act of foot washing a mini-kenosis because Jesus, so to speak, temporarily emptied himself of his Lord-like and Master-like prerogatives and dignity. He dressed like a servant and then did a servant's job. Of course we do not see here the kind of ontological kenosis that is discussed in this book, namely, the Logos divesting itself of certain divine properties in order to become a human being. What we see in John 13 is a kind of moral kenosis, namely, a master voluntarily taking on the role of a slave. Still, centuries of Christians have been gripped by this simple story. The religious power inherent in this act of love and humility is precisely one of the points that makes kenosis so compelling to those who defend it.

## 2

Those who reject kenosis do so for a great variety of reasons. But perhaps the most important of them is the idea that kenosis is inconsistent with the most exalted notions of God or with our deepest philosophical intuitions about God. Usually the debate revolves around such traditional divine properties as immutability, impassibility, and greatness. . . .

Does kenosis conflict with our deepest convictions about God? At this point, it seems, we quickly reach an impasse. Who is more exalted, more God-like, more worthy of worship—a God who can or a God who cannot undergo change? Or—a God who can or a God who cannot undergo self-limitation? Or, to ask the question in Anselmian terms, which God is *greater*? Opinions will obviously differ here. . . .

We believe that some resist a kenotic understanding of the Incarnate Christ because of a fear that such a view will erode his divinity. . . .

However, it is worth paying a little more attention to what one might call the supernatural dimension of the portrait of Jesus given in the gospels. It is true, as kenoticists wish to stress, that Jesus sometimes appears finite in his knowledge and power. However, it is also true that in the gospels Jesus frequently performs miracles and possesses knowledge that an ordinary human would not possess. An excellent example would be the story in John 4, in which Jesus tells a Samaritan woman, whom he has apparently never met before, that the man she has referred to as her husband is not really her husband, though she has had five different husbands (John 4:17). If Jesus has put aside such properties as omniscience and omnipotence, how can he have such knowledge and perform such miracles as calming the storm in Luke 8:19–25?

Kenoticists are in no way uncomfortable with the supernatural dimension that Jesus exhibits here and in many other places, but they explain this dimension by pointing to another fundamental characteristic of the biblical portrait: Jesus lived his life in complete dependence upon and in complete union with the Father and the Spirit. When Jesus performs a miracle, on a kenotic view of the Incarnation, he does not suddenly draw upon a hidden "power-pack" of divine properties that he has been holding in reserve all along, to be pulled out on special occasions. Rather, he draws upon the power of the Father through a life lived in the Spirit. We believe that it is crucially important to notice, in the context of a discussion of kenosis, an obvious but often overlooked fact, namely, that Jesus lived his life in complete and continuous dependence on the Holy Spirit and that he lived a life of perfect submission to the Father.

Interestingly, it is in John's gospel, the book that gives the clearest portrait of Jesus as divine, that this dependence on the Father and Spirit is emphasized most strongly. For example, in John 6:38 Jesus says that he has come not to do his own will but "to do the will of him who sent me." In John 7:16 Jesus says that "my teaching is not my own. It comes from him who sent me." In John 10:18 Jesus says that he intends to lay down his life because of the "command I received from my Father." Jesus performs the mighty miracle of the raising of Lazarus in John 11, but does so by first praying to the Father, thanking the Father that he always hears Jesus. In John 14:10 Jesus tells us that the Father lives in him and that the work Jesus does is really the work the Father is doing through him. And in John 17:5, Jesus shows his dependence upon the Father by his prayer that the Father would glorify him with the glory that Jesus had with the Father "before the world began," the glory that Jesus has willingly given up to become incarnate as a human being.

So there is no contradiction at all between the supernatural dimension of Jesus' earthly life and a kenotic account of the Incarnation. In fact, the kenotic account highlights the deep unity between Father, Son, and Spirit that endures throughout the Incarnation, and emphasizes the way a truly human Jesus as the Son of God provides a model for us of how human life is to be lived. For we too can live our lives in dependence upon the Father and in union with the Spirit, and thus be united to Christ as well. Even the miracles Jesus performs do not separate him from humanity; in fact, he explicitly tells his disciples that if they have faith they will have access to the same miraculous power he himself has shown: "I tell you the truth, anyone who has faith in me will do what I have been doing. He will do even greater things than these, because I am going to the Father" (John 14:12).

## 3.3 The Significance of Incarnation

*Karl Barth*, Church Dogmatics, *IV/1*, The Doctrine of Reconciliation, *trans. G. W. Bromiley (Edinburgh: T. & T. Clark, 1974), 186–88*

Who God is and what it is to be divine is something we have to learn where God has revealed Himself and His nature, the essence of the divine. And if He has revealed Himself in Jesus Christ as the God who does this, it is not for us to be wiser than He and to say that it is in contradiction with the divine essence. We have to be ready to be taught by Him that we have been too small and perverted in our thinking about Him within the framework of a false idea of God. It is not for us to speak of a contradiction and rift in the being of God, but to learn to correct our notions of the being of God, to reconstitute them in the light of the fact that He does this. We may believe that God can and must only be absolute in contrast to all that is relative, exalted in contrast to all that is lowly, active in contrast to all suffering, inviolable in contrast to all temptation, transcendent in contrast to all immanence, and therefore divine in contrast to everything human, in short that He can and must be only the "Wholly Other." But such beliefs are shown to be quite untenable, and corrupt and pagan, by the fact that God does in fact be and do this in Jesus Christ. We cannot make them the standard by which to measure what God can or cannot do, or the basis of the judgment that in doing this He brings Himself into self-contradiction. By doing this God proves to us that He can do it, that to do it is within His nature. And He shows Himself to be more great and rich and sovereign than we had ever imagined. And our ideas of His nature must be guided by this, and not *vice versa*.

We have to think something after the following fashion. As God was in Christ, far from being against Himself, or at disunity with Himself, He has put into effect the freedom of His divine love, the love in which He is divinely free. He has therefore done and revealed that which corresponds to His divine nature. His immutability does not stand in the way of this. It must not be denied, but this possibility is included in His unalterable being. He is absolute, infinite, exalted, active, impassible, transcendent, but in all this He is the One who loves in freedom, the One who is free in His love, and therefore not His own prisoner. He is all this as the Lord, and in such a way that He embraces the opposites of these concepts even while He is superior to them. He is all this as the Creator, who has created the world as the reality distinct from Himself but willed and affirmed by Him and therefore as His world, as the world which belongs to Him, in relation to which He can be God and act as God in an absolute way and also a relative, in an infinite and also a finite, in an exalted and also a lowly, in an active and also a passive, in a transcendent and also an immanent, and finally, in a divine and also a human—indeed, in relation to which He Himself can become worldly, making His own both its form, the *forma servi*, and also its cause; and all without giving up His own form, the *forma Dei*, and His own glory, but adopting the form and cause of man into the most perfect communion with His own, accepting solidarity with the world. God can do this. And no limit is set to His ability to do it by the contradiction of the creature against Him. It does not escape Him by turning to that which is not and losing itself in it, for, although he is not the Creator of that which is not, He is its sovereign Lord. It corresponds to and is grounded in His divine nature that in free grace He should be faithful to the unfaithful creature who has not deserved it and who would inevitably perish without it, that in relation to it He should establish that communion between His own form and cause and that of the creature, that He should make His own its being in contradiction and under the consequences of that contradiction, that He should maintain His covenant in relation to sinful man (not surrendering His deity, for how could that help? But giving up and sacrificing Himself), and in that way supremely asserting Himself and His deity. His particular, and highly particularised, presence in grace, in which the eternal Word descended to the lowest parts of the earth (Eph. 4:9) and tabernacled in the man Jesus (Jn. 1:14), dwelling in this one man in the fulness of His Godhead (Col. 2:9), is itself the demonstration and exercise of His omnipresence, i.e., of the perfection in which He has His own place which is superior to all the places created by Him, not excluding but including all other places. His omnipotence is that of a divine plenitude of power in the fact that (as opposed to any abstract omnipotence) it can assume the form of weakness and impotence and do so as omnipotence, triumphing in this form. The eternity in which He Himself is true time and the Creator of all time is revealed in the fact that, although our time is that of sin and death, He can enter it and Himself be temporal in it, yet without ceasing to be eternal, able rather to be the Eternal in time. His wisdom does not deny itself, but proclaims itself in what necessarily appears folly to the world; His right-eousness in ranging Himself with the unrighteous as One who is accused with them, as the first, and properly the only One to come under accusa-tion; His Holiness in having mercy on man, in taking his misery to heart, in willing to share it with him in order to take it away from him. God does not have to dishonour Himself when He goes into the far country, and conceals His glory. For He is truly honoured in this concealment. This concealment, and therefore His condescension as such, is the image and reflection in which we see Him as He is. His glory is the freedom of the love which He exercises and reveals in all this. In this respect it differs from the unfree and loveless glory of all the gods imagined by man. Every-thing depends on our seeing it, and in it the true and majestic nature of God: not trying to construct it arbitrarily; but deducing it from its reve-lation in the divine nature of Jesus Christ. From this we learn that the *forma Dei* consists in the grace in which God Himself assumes and makes His own the *forma servi*. We have to hold fast to this without being dis-turbed or confused by any pictures of false gods. It is this that we have to see and honour and worship as the mystery of the deity of Christ—not an ontic and inward divine paradox, the postulate of which has its basis only in our own very real contradiction against God and the false ideas of God which correspond to it.

*Jürgen Moltmann,* The Crucified God, *trans. R. A. Wilson and John Bowden (London: SCM Press, 1974), 87–88, 92*

Every question presupposes a context in which the question arises. . . .

. . . In antiquity the divine being was not a problem. Its existence was rarely doubted. It was man in his relationship to God which was the prob-lem. The next step was from the general question of God to the mystery of Jesus. Was the eternal, unchangeable God revealed in Jesus? . . .

Since the Renaissance, the Enlightenment and the rise of modern tech-nology, the relationship between man and nature in most fields has been reversed. Man is no longer dependent upon uncomprehended forces in nature and history, recognizing in this dependence his total reliance on the gods or on God. Instead, nature and history have become increasingly dependent upon man. The problem of modern man is no longer so much how he can live with gods and demons but how he can survive with the bomb, revolution and destruction of the balance of nature. He usurps more and more of nature and takes it under his control. The vital ques-tion for him, therefore, is how this world which he has usurped can be humanized. His main problem is no longer the universal finitude which he experiences in solidarity with all other creatures, but the humanity of his own world.

Thus the christological question is no longer, "Is the eternal God in Christ?", but "Can Jesus be called God, and in what respect and how far is he divine?" Thus from the time of Lessing to the present day the vital question of humanity has for many become the main question about Christ.

*Jürgen Moltmann*, The Trinity and the Kingdom of God, *trans. Margaret Kohl (London: SCM Press, 1981), 118–19*

In the incarnation of the Son the triune God enters into the limited, finite situation. Not only does he enter into this state of being man; he accepts and adopts it himself, making it part of his own, eternal life. He becomes *the human* God.

If this is the meaning which is inherent in the incarnation of the Son as such, then God's self-humiliation is completed and perfected in the passion and death of Jesus the Son. Here too an indwelling significance is perceptible: God does not merely enter into the finitude of men and women; he enters into the situation of their sin and God-forsakenness as well. He does not merely enter into this situation; he also accepts and adopts it himself, making it part of his own eternal life. The kenosis is realized on the cross. Of course it serves the reconciliation and redemption of men and women, but it also contains in itself this other significance: God becomes the God who identifies himself with men and women to the point of death, and beyond. The incarnation of the Son is not something transitional. It is and remains to all eternity. There is no God other than the incarnate, human God who is one with men and women.

The *outward incarnation* presupposes *inward self-humiliation*. That is why the incarnation intervenes in the inner relations of the Trinity.

Again we can make this clear from the image of love. Love that communicates itself requires response if it is to find bliss. But from his image in the world the Father can only expect the love that is a free response; and in order to make this free response possible, love must concede freedom and offer freedom to the beloved. In order to experience the free response it desires, love must wait patiently. It cannot compel a response by violence. For the sake of freedom, and the love responded to in freedom, God limits and empties himself. He withdraws his omnipotence because he has confidence in the free response of men and women.

God does not encounter men and women "as God"; he encounters them in human form, in the incarnate and crucified Son. With respect to God's omnipotence this means a limitation. But with respect to God's goodness it is a de-limitation. His strength is made perfect in weakness. The traditional doctrine about God's kenosis has always looked at just the one aspect of God's self-limitation, self-emptying and self-humiliation. It has overlooked the other side: God's limitations inwardly are de-limitations outwards. God is nowhere greater than in his humiliation. God is nowhere more glorious than in his impotence. God is nowhere more divine than when he becomes man.

*Karl Barth,* The Humanity of God, *trans. John Newton Thomas and Thomas Wieser (London: Collins, 1961), 46–49*

It is when we look at Jesus Christ that we know decisively that God's deity does not exclude, but includes His *humanity*. . . .

It is not as though God stands in need of another as His partner, and in particular of man, in order to be truly God. "What is man, that thou art mindful of him, and the son of man that thou dost care for him?" [Ps. 8:4.] Why should God not also be able, as eternal Love, to be sufficient unto Himself? In His life as Father, Son, and Holy Spirit He would in truth be no lonesome, no egotistical God even without man, yes, even without the whole created universe. And He must more than ever be not *for* man; He *could*—one even thinks He *must*—rather be against him. But in that is the mystery in which he meets us in the existence of Jesus Christ. He wants in His freedom actually not to be without man but *with* him and in the same freedom not against him but *for* him, and that apart from or even counter to what man deserves. He wants in fact to be man's partner, his almighty and compassionate Saviour. He chooses to give man the benefit of His power, which encompasses not only the high and the distant but also the deep and the near, in order to maintain communion with him in the realm guaranteed by His deity. He determines to love him, to be his God, his Lord, his compassionate Preserver and Saviour to eternal life, and to desire his praise and service.

In this divinely free volition and election, in this sovereign decision (the ancients said, in His decree), God is *human*. His free affirmation of man, His free concern for him, His free substitution for him—this is God's humanity. We recognise it exactly at the point where we also first recognise His deity. Is it not true that in Jesus Christ, as He is attested in the Holy Scripture, genuine deity includes in itself genuine humanity? There is the father who cares for his lost son, the king who does the same for his insolvent debtor, the Samaritan who takes pity on the one who fell among robbers and in his thorough-going act of compassion cares for him in a fashion as unexpected as it is liberal. And this is the act of compassion to which all these parables as parables of the Kingdom of heaven refer. The very One who speaks in these parables takes to His heart the weakness and the perversity, the helplessness and the misery, of the human race surrounding Him. He does not despise men, but in an inconceivable manner esteems them highly just as they are, takes them in to His heart and sets Himself in their place. He perceives that the superior will of God, to which He wholly subordinates Himself, requires that He sacrifice Himself for the human race, and seeks His honour in doing this. In the mirror of this humanity of Jesus Christ the humanity of God enclosed in His deity reveals itself. Thus God is as He is. Thus He affirms man. Thus He is concerned about him. Thus He stands up for him.

### 3.4 Revelation, Evidence, and Meaning

*David A. Pailin, "The Incarnation as a Continuing Reality,"*
Religious Studies *6 (1970): 306–7, 319–20, 326*

Some people . . . may want to argue that an incarnational event is basic to faith, solely on the grounds that it only shows that God knows from his own experience what it is to be a man and so can be trusted as one who "understands" our plight. Some interpretations of the doctrine of the Ascension seem to follow this interpretation when they regard that doctrine as expressing the incorporation of human experiences within the Godhead. In so far as such a doctrine presupposes that the precise quality of human experience is not available to God apart from an historical "incarnation" in which God actually "becomes" a man (however this is understood), I find it quite unacceptable since it imposes a limitation on the eternal, sympathetic love of God which I cannot see to be justified. Certainly I am limited in my awareness of your experience or of the experience of a dog. Two people in love, however, will claim that as they increasingly love each other so they increasingly become sympathetically aware of each other's feelings and experiences. Must we not, then, allow that God, whose knowledge can be seen as derived from unlimitedly sympathetic love and awareness of others, so truly "knows" us as we are without loss and error that there can be no part of human experience that is closed to him? If this is the case, the view of the Incarnation which sees it as making certain experiences available to God is based on far too limited an understanding of what is meant by God's knowledge.

A second view is that the incarnation is necessary for God to enable himself to effect an atonement with men. For instance, it is claimed that an incarnation of God was needed to produce a perfect man to offer the perfect sacrifice which is the condition of atonement. This view seems to me also indefensible since it presumes that God is so limited—by the "red-tape" demands of his purity and justice and honour—that he cannot do what he wants simply because he wants it and because it is good. If God desires the reconciliation of man with himself, he does not need an incarnatory event to make it possible so far as he is concerned. Thus I suggest that views of the incarnation which see its significance in what it does for God (or what God does for himself) rest upon unacceptably inadequate concepts of God. But if incarnation is not doing something for God, can we understand its central theological significance in terms of what it makes possible for man?

A third possible interpretation of incarnation is that it makes possible for man an understanding of his authentic existence by providing him with an actual example of it. This interpretation seems to me to be deficient if it turns the "God" who is "incarnated" into "man's ideal for man" and denies any grounding for that ideal to exist outside man. What we are being offered in that case is not anything that has to do with "God" in any basic theistic sense . . . but something that tells us about the "ideals" which a man must actualise in his own existence if he is to find authentic life. Now it may be argued that this is the function of Christ in the Christian faith: if so I suggest that what we are given is a human Jesus who is set before us as the ideal "man for others" or "man in dependence upon God" or "man open to the future" and has no reference to anything other than man. It is not a Jesus of which the notion of "incarnation" is properly predicable *unless*—and this is a vital "unless"—such an ideal human life *also* is to be understood as expressing in some way or other something of the nature of God.

This brings us to the fourth interpretation of what it means to talk about incarnation. This is the view that such talk is claiming that in the events so described we are given a *revelation* of the nature of God. It is, for example, not just a perfect human life that we are presented with but a human life in which we are given knowledge of the *actual* nature of God, a knowledge on which we base our religious faith, our attitude to and our interpretation of the whole of reality. . . .

The view that the function of an incarnational claim is to provide insight into the nature of God does not seem to me to be open to the objections that can be made against the other views of the incarnation, namely that they depend upon inadequate understandings of God. . . .

On the other hand, such a "revelatory" view of incarnation may seem to be open to the objection that an incarnation must be redundant since it provides us with a knowledge of God that must be already presupposed in our decision that here we have a revelation of God. For example, it may be held that we claim that the life of Jesus is a revelatory incarnation of God because it is a life of self-giving love and because we know—or believe we know—already that self-giving love is the character of God. Thus what incarnational claims do is not to give us new knowledge of God but rather concrete examples of his nature—examples which we choose because they are in accordance with our existing views about God. . . .

But consider cases where I am unable to be present in person but arrange for a substitute to act for me. If I give this substitute very precise instructions about my wishes and if he carries them out extremely faithfully and conscientiously, could not people watching *him* claim with reason that they now understood *me*? Can we not use this analogically of God and Jesus? If God called the man Jesus to act according to his will in every situation and if Jesus, through unbroken relationship with God, completely grasped the character of that will and expressed it, would it not be valid to claim that in Jesus' acts we perceive the active actuality of God within the limits imposed by human life? The mode of incarnation is thus interpreted as a vocation for Jesus to be perfectly at one with God and a vocation which he perfectly fulfilled. He was a man, with all the limitations and freedom of a man, but in completely responding to God's call to him, he "incarnated" God's active actuality.

Probably the main objection to this view is that since all men are called to fulfil the will of God, it seems to deny the uniqueness of Jesus. Two replies may be offered to this criticism. First, since Jesus fulfilled that vocation perfectly, he may properly be regarded as unique. In no other is the will of God perfectly expressed. Secondly, there is no reason why on this interpretation Jesus' vocation should not be regarded as a unique one—that he was called to express God's actuality in ways to which others are not called. . . .

In the end, it is not, it seems to me, the factuality of the event nor the accuracy of the record of the event but the truth of the insight into ultimate reality which it arouses that is important. The stories which arouse insight may not correspond to what actually happened. This is not important if, like parables, they lead us to perceive what is *actually* happening at the level of God and ultimate reality. This is the *factuality* that is vital: not the factuality of the story which provides the insight. At the same time, let me say that I recognise that something, some occurrence, must have aroused the insight and, furthermore, that I am fully prepared to allow that as a matter of historical probability it is highly unlikely that the reports which we have of the life of Jesus do not fairly well correspond to the events which did lead to the Christian insight into the nature of God. What I do want to claim, however, is that it is not these contingent facts that in the end are the facts vital to belief. The facts that are indispensable to belief are the facts of a quite different level of reality which concern how God is actually active. This is the factual element on which faith depends. The work, then, of the historian and New Testament critic is very interesting but ultimately it does not provide us with the facts on which faith depends: it only helps us to understand what evoked insight into those facts among the first Christians.

*Austin Farrer, "Christ is God," in* Austin Farrer: The Essential Sermons, *ed. Leslie Houlden (London: SPCK, 1991), 35*

The evidence, then, that Jesus was God-from-God and God-with-God, was that a life had come into the world which gave back to God the picture of his own face, and the love of his own heart. And the second evidence was the power of it. By union with this life men received a share in something not human at all, an eternal divine sonship. "To as many as received him he gave the power to become sons of God, to them that believe on his name; who not of blood, nor of the will of the flesh, nor of the will of man, but of God were begotten." He could not give us a share of what he had not got; before all adopted sonship like ours, comes the true natural sonship which is his.

We have then to consider in Christ primarily what he claims, what he is, what he does to us. There are also supporting evidences of an exterior kind preceding, accompanying and following his earthly life.

The evidence preceding his advent is the remarkable history of Israel, a nation distinguished from all others and held together by nothing but the faith that God would establish his Kingdom through this people. Now, in a way that is far too various and too complete to be described here, Jesus fulfilled all the strands of prophetic hope; not in a soulless, mechanical way, but in a divine, living and unpredictable way. Such a preparation for Christ, and such a fulfilment in Christ seems a work truly worthy of God.

The evidence accompanying his earthly life is his miracles. Spiritual men have at all times done wonderful things; if Christ had not done any it would have surprised us. His divine nature is not proved by his miracles, but it is confirmed by them. Antiquity was credulous, and the evidence is difficult to sift; but only stubborn prejudice will deny that Jesus was a worker of wonders, and more especially that his mighty acts slipped from him like the running over of a divine power which could not be hidden. He did not exert himself to do miracles, still less to exhibit them.

The evidence succeeding his earthly life is his resurrection. His friends were convinced by it immediately, and turned into a believing church by it. His enemies never claimed that they possessed or could exhibit his body. The resurrection sealed the Father's acceptance of the Son's supreme sacrifice.

Last of all we may put what we will call retrospective evidence. When the disciples came to look back and ask how the divine Saviour had come into the world, the answer was, By a divine and virginal birth. Faith will accept this retrospective evidence as in agreement with what faith already believes, and as something divinely appropriate.

*Austin Farrer, "Incarnation," in* The Brink of Mystery
*(London: SPCK, 1976), 20–21*

What did Jesus know? He knew, initially, what a village boy learnt, who listened to the Rabbis, and made the best of his opportunities. But of this knowledge, scanty as we should think it, he made a divinely perfect use. It became in his head the alphabet of ideas through which the spirit within him spelt out the truth of what he was, and what he had to do. He was not saved from factual errors in matters irrelevant: he was not prevented from supposing that Moses wrote the whole Pentateuch, or that the world had begun five thousand years ago. But he saw in detail day by day with an unerring eye how to be a true Son to his Father, and a true saviour of his people. He walked in factual darkness by spiritual light; where knowledge was not available, love and candour steered him through. He never judged wrong on the evidence he had; he discerned between good and evil, and marked us out the path of life. He started, like the rest of us, from nowhere—from a germ in the womb; he found the whole truth, through death and resurrection.

When one speaks of incarnation . . . one is expected, perhaps, to speak of Christ's virginal birth. But the virginal birth is not the substance of the incarnation; it is the peculiar way in which (we have been told) it pleased God to bring it about. Jesus is not the Son of God *because* he had no human father. It would have been conceivable, though it did not happen, that the Son of God might have become incarnate as the offspring of an ordinary union.

I would ask you to observe the manner in which our evangelists view the miracle of Christ's birth. Jesus, they say, is the divinely given heir and son of Joseph; his descent is always reckoned through him, never through Mary. But he was a son whom Joseph did nothing to get. Zachariah's getting of John Baptist was what he could not do without God's special aid; Joseph's getting of Jesus was something he did not do at all, it was wholly the work of God. God, who can of the very stones raise up children to Abraham, and who, when Jesus was dead in the sepulchre, raised him to immortal life; God, to whom the disciples of Jesus come, every time they pray, asking for the miracle of a new birth: this God first brought Jesus forth from the virginity of Mary, displaying the unmerited and sovereign freedom of his grace: who made the world where no world was, who wonderfully ordained the excellence of man's estate, and yet more wonderfully has restored it.

*J. Gresham Machen,* The Virgin Birth of Christ
*(London: James Clarke, 1958), 380–81, 395*

Even in isolation, indeed, the story of the virgin birth should give the thoughtful historian pause. There is a startling beauty and vividness and originality about the first chapters of Matthew and Luke. Only superficiality can detect a similarity here to the coarse and degrading stories which are found in the surrounding world. Whence came this supremely beautiful tale, so unlike the products of human fancy, so unlike the myths of all the peoples that have lived upon the earth? Whence came such a story not in later generations, but in close proximity to the time of the narrated events? Whence came the self-evidencing quality of this narrative, so simple yet so profound?

These questions, we think, are unanswerable. Even if the story of the virgin birth stood alone, it would at least present an insoluble problem to the [one] who would regard it as untrue. But it would be hard for this bewilderment to issue in belief. The story of the virgin birth is the story of a stupendous miracle, and against any such thing there is an enormous presumption drawn from the long experience of the race.

As it is, however, that presumption can be overcome; it can be overcome when the tradition of the virgin birth is removed from its isolation and taken in connection with the whole glorious picture of the One who in this tradition is said to be virgin-born. . . .

Moreover, the knowledge of the virgin birth is important because of its bearing upon our view of the solidarity of the race in the guilt and power of sin. If we hold a Pelagian view of sin, we shall be little interested in the virgin birth of our Lord; we shall have little difficulty in understanding how a sinless One could be born as other men are born. But if we believe, as the Bible teaches, that all mankind are under an awful curse, then we shall rejoice in knowing that there entered into the sinful race from the outside One upon whom the curse did not rest save as He bore it for those whom He redeemed by His blood.

How, except by the virgin birth, could our Saviour have lived a complete human life from the mother's womb, and yet have been from the very beginning no product of what had gone before, but a supernatural Person come into the world from the outside to redeem the sinful race? We may not, indeed, set limits to the power of God; we cannot say what God might or might not have done. Yet we can say at least that no other way can be conceived by us.

*Brian Hebblethwaite, "The Moral and Religious Value of the Incarnation,"*
*in* Incarnation and Myth, *ed. Michael Goulder*
*(London: SCM Press, 1979), 92–95*

What, then, is the moral and religious value of the incarnation? I shall first summarize this under four headings: (a) revelation and personal knowledge of God; (b) trinitarian belief; (c) the problem of evil and the atonement; (d) presence and participation.

(a) In the first place, the moral and religious value of the incarnation lies in the greatly increased potential for human knowledge of God and personal union with God introduced by God's own presence and acts, in human form, this side of the gap between Creator and creature. The character of Christ *is* for us the revealed character of God, and becomes the criterion for our understanding of the nature and will of God. In a sense the humanity of Christ mediates God to us, but in another sense God's love is communicated to us immediately by God's own incarnate presence here in our midst. It is perfectly true that we today are not face to face with God incarnate as the disciples were. But the inevitable limitations of that particularity are overcome, as I shall stress below, by his spiritual and sacramental presence and activity, by means of which God's personal self-revelation in Jesus is universalized. My point here is that the story of Jesus gives that universal activity of God its concrete, particular and utterly personal form.

The humanity of Christ is, of course, for Christian understanding, permanently taken into God. The risen Christ remains the focus and channel of our knowledge of God and the key by which all other experience of God is converted into personal knowledge of the blessed Trinity.

(b) The trinitarian implications of christology must be stressed further here, if we are to avoid an excessively individualized Jesus cult. Jesus reveals God to us, not only by his character and acts and passion, but also by his prayers to the Father, by his resurrection, and by the outpouring of the Spirit. But the doctrine of the Trinity has an independent place, as well, in our assessment of the moral and religious value of incarnational christology. For in forcing us to think of God in richer, relational terms, as the fullness of love given and love received within his own being prior to creation, it resolves that impasse in pure monotheism which results from conceiving of God on the analogy of an isolated individual. Lampe claims that there is no need to project relationship into God, since God participates immanently in his creatures' reciprocities. But this makes creation necessary to God, if God is to enjoy the fullness of being as love. This, I submit, is to introduce real incoherence into any religiously and metaphysically satisfying concept of God.

(c) Thirdly, the moral and religious value of the incarnation is seen in the way it confronts the world's evil. . . . The moral force of this depends on Christ's *being* God. One cannot accept responsibility for the world's ills through someone else. . . . Only if we can say that God has *himself*, on the cross, "borne our sorrows" can we find him universally present "in" the sufferings of others. It is not a question of "awareness" and "sympathy". It is, as Whitehead put it, a matter of the "fellow-sufferer who understands". This whole dimension of the Christian doctrine of the incarnation, its recognition of the costly nature of God's forgiving love, and its perception that only a suffering God is morally credible, is lost if God's involvement is reduced to a matter of "awareness" and "sympathy".

I come, thus somewhat indirectly, to the doctrine of the atonement, which, of course, has traditionally been held to spell out the chief moral and religious value of the incarnation. As J. K. Mozley emphasized in his excellent essay in *Mysterium Christi* on "Christology and Soteriology", it is soteriological considerations that require us to think of Jesus as coming to the world from the side of God, and not as the highest stage in religious evolution. And certainly it is only if we can think of Jesus Christ as being divine as well as being human that we can speak of his life and death and resurrection as of universal salvific significance for all men. The objectivity of the atonement consists in its being God's act for all. Unfortunately the manner in which this is so has been spelled out in a variety of theories of the atonement which are themselves open to grave moral objections, and this has led to revulsion from objective theories of the atonement and a failure to perceive the real moral significance of the incarnation. Consequently it needs to be stated quite categorically that God's forgiving love does not depend on the death of Christ, but rather is manifested and enacted in it. It is precisely because the Spirit who converts our hearts and builds up our life in the Spirit is the Spirit of the crucified God that God's forgiveness and our reconciliation have the profoundly moral quality that has been the real inspiration of Christian piety down the ages, despite its often crude forms of expression. The costly and deeply moral nature of God's reconciling work was summarized by Austin Farrer thus:

> What, then, did God do for his people's redemption? He came amongst them, bringing his kingdom, and he let events take their human course. He set the divine life in human neighbourhood. Men discovered it in struggling with it and were captured by it [in] crucifying it. (*Saving Belief*, London, Hodder & Stoughton, 1967, p. 99)

(d) Fourthly, the religious value of the incarnation is seen in the christological and trinitarian concentration in terms of which present Christian experience, worship and life are to be understood. As Moule has repeatedly stressed, it is conviction of Christ as a living presence, both spiritually and sacramentally, that differentiates specifically Christian awareness of God from all other. Moreover Christian worship has never been conceived solely as a matter of response, in gratitude and adoration, by creatures to their Creator. It is rather a matter of being caught up into Christ's eternal offering to the Father, and of being indwelt by the Spirit, who, from within, draws us in worship into the inner life of God. Similarly, in the body of Christ, we become, by adoption and grace, instruments in the history of divine action, which is not only a matter of God's movement out towards his creation, but a movement back from creation to God. The specifically Christian insight is that this too, the movement from creation to God, takes place in God, through the humanity of Christ, and derivatively through ourselves, as we are united with Christ, alike in worship and work.

## Topics for Discussion

1. Is it possible for us to make sense today of the decision of the Council of Chalcedon in 451 to declare Christ to be two natures in one person, both fully God and fully man?
2. To what extent have the christological questions for today changed since Chalcedon? Is this purely the result of biblical criticism, or are other factors involved as well?
3. What is entailed by kenosis, or self-emptying? Is it simply a device for explaining why Jesus made mistakes (e.g., about the end of the world), or are larger issues at stake, such as what it is to be human, and what it is for God to give us real freedom?
4. What objections are commonly raised against the notion of kenosis? How adequately might they be answered?
5. Does it matter whether Jesus was God incarnate or not? Which other Christian doctrines would be affected if non-incarnational views were to be adopted?

# Chapter Four

# A Christ for All?

## 4.1 Christologies of Liberation

*Juan Luis Segundo*, Liberation of Theology, *trans. John Drury (Maryknoll, NY: Orbis Books, 1976), 3*

What will remain of the "theology of liberation" in a few short years? The question may seem to be pessimistic in tone, suggesting that liberation theology was a superficial thing or a passing fad. That is certainly not the case. My question should be approached in a positive and hopeful spirit.

It is my opinion that the "theology of liberation," however well or poorly the name fits, represents a point of no return in Latin America. It is an irreversible thrust in the Christian process of creating a new consciousness and maturity in our faith. Countless Christians have committed themselves to a fresh and radical interpretation of their faith, to a new re-experiencing of it in their real lives. And they have done this not only as isolated individuals but also as influential and sizeable groups within the Church.

While the process is irreversible, it is also broad in scope and varied within itself. Therefore it is not easy to say what the exact content of the theology of liberation is for all the Christians involved in it. Certain basic points, however, are clearly shared by all. They would maintain that the longstanding stress on individual salvation in the next world represents a distortion of Jesus' message. He was concerned with man's full and integral liberation, a process which is already at work in history and which makes use of historical means. They would maintain that the Church does not posses any sort of magical effectiveness where salvation is concerned but rather liberating factors in its faith and its liturgy; that the victory of the Church must be viewed in functional terms rather than quantitative or numerical terms, insofar as the Church's specific and proper means manage to exercise a truly powerful impact on human history. They would also maintain that there are not two separate orders—one being a supernatural order outside history and the other being a natural order inside history; that instead one and the same grace raises human beings to a supernatural level and provides them with the means they need to achieve their true destiny within one and the same historical process.

*Leonardo Boff, OFM,* Jesus Christ Liberator, *trans. Patrick Hughes (London, SPCK, 1980), 289–91*

When Jesus embraces death of his own free will, he reveals the total freedom of himself and his projects. He points up one concrete way of fleshing out the reality of God's kingdom when he accepts death out of love, maintains his fellowship with the downtrodden of history, pardons those who have afflicted him, and puts himself into God's hands in the face of historical failure.

The motives behind the assassination of Jesus are two-fold. Both have something to do with the structural level. First of all, Jesus was condemned as a *blasphemer.* He presents a God who is different from the God of the status quo. As Jon Sobrino points out, Jesus unmasked the religious hypocrisy of the standing order and its use of God to justify injustice. In that sense the religious authorities were correct in saying that Jesus was preaching a God opposed to their own.

Secondly, his whole attitude and approach was eminently liberative. . . . Thus the political authorities accused him of being a *guerrilla fighter* and executed him for that. His preaching and his outlook brought him close to the liberation project of the Zealots. After all, he looked for the imminent arrival of the kingdom; he acted in radical ways; he made inflammatory remarks about the violent bearing away the kingdom; he acted freely vis-à-vis the established imperial authorities; and he clearly exercised leadership over the common people, who wanted to make him their chief. On the other hand Jesus clearly moved away from the spirit and approach of the Zealots. He renounced the religious messianism of a political cast. Messianism grounded on the use of force and power would not succeed in concretizing the kingdom, he felt. The kingdom entails a more radical liberation, one that gets beyond the breakdown of brotherhood and calls for the creation of new human beings.

The cross demonstrates the conflict-ridden nature of every process of liberation undertaken when the structure of injustice has gained the upper hand. Under such conditions liberation can come about only through martyrdom and sacrifice on behalf of others and God's cause in the world. That is the route which Jesus consciously chose and accepted. . . .

The resurrection of the crucified Jesus shows that it is not meaningless to die for other human beings and God. In Jesus' resurrection, light is shed on the anonymous death of all those who have lost out in history while fighting for the cause of justice and ultimate human meaningfulness. As one author [F. Belo] suggests, "the question of resurrection is rightly posed from the standpoint of insurrection". The resurrection tells us that the murderer shall not triumph over his victim.

*Libertatis Nuntius, X, 3–7*
*(In* Instruction on Certain Aspects of the "Theology of Liberation,"
*by the Sacred Congregation for the Doctrine of the Faith*
*[London: Catholic Truth Society, 1984], 26–27)*

*This is an extract from the first official response to liberation theology from the Roman Catholic Church's Sacred Congregation for the Doctrine of the Faith, over which Cardinal Joseph Ratzinger (now Pope Benedict XVI) presided.*

It becomes very difficult, not to say impossible, to engage in a real dialogue with some "theologians of liberation" in such a way that the other participant is listened to, and his arguments are discussed with objectivity and attention. For these theologians start out with the idea, more or less consciously, that the viewpoint of the oppressed and revolutionary class, which is their own, is the single true point of view. Theological criteria for truth are thus relativized and subordinated to the imperatives of the class struggle. In this perspective, *orthodoxy* or the right rule of faith, is substituted by the notion of *orthopraxy* as the criterion of the truth. In this connection it is important not to confuse practical orientation, which is proper to traditional theology in the same way that speculative orientation is, with the recognized and privileged priority given to a certain type of *praxis*. For them, this praxis is the revolutionary *praxis* which thus becomes the supreme criterion for theological truth. A healthy theological method no doubt will always take the *praxis* of the Church into account and will find there one of its foundations, but that is because that praxis comes from the faith and is a lived expression of it.

For the "theologies of liberation" however, the social doctrine of the Church is rejected with disdain. It is said that it comes from the illusion of a possible compromise, typical of the middle class which has no historic destiny.

The new *hermeneutic* inherent in the "theologies of liberation" leads to an essentially *political* re-reading of the Scriptures. Thus, a major importance is given to the *Exodus* event inasmuch as it is a liberation from political servitude. Likewise, a political reading of the *Magnificat* is proposed. The mistake here is not in bringing attention to a political dimension of the readings of Scripture, but in making of this one dimension the principal or exclusive component. This leads to a reductionist reading of the Bible.

Likewise, one places oneself within the perspective of a temporal messianism, which is one of the most radical of the expressions of secularization of the Kingdom of God and of its absorption into the immanence of human history.

In giving such priority to the political dimension, one is led to deny the *radical newness* of the New Testament and above all to misunderstand the person of Our Lord Jesus Christ, true God and true man, and thus the specific character of the salvation he gave us, that is above all liberation from sin, which is the source of all evils.

*Hans Urs von Balthasar, "Liberation Theology in the Light of Salvation History," trans. Erasmus Leiva, in* Liberation Theology in Latin America, *ed. James V. Schall, SJ (San Francisco: Ignatius Press, 1982), 145–46*

At the Medellín Bishops' Conference there was much talk of *estructuras injustas y opresoras* ["unjust and oppressive structures"], of *situación de injusticia* ["situation of injustice"] and *situación de pecado* ["situation of sin"]. Now, societal situations can be unjust, but in themselves they cannot be sinful. Only those persons can be sinful who are responsible for the existence of such situations and who continue to tolerate them even though they could abolish or ameliorate them.

The New Testament basically recognizes only two contrasting forms of existence: the one subject to *hamartia* ["sin"] and the other freed from *hamartia* by Christ. It does not, therefore, appear to give a direct answer to the question of how Christians can and should live within worldly structures which, even in the best of cases, are only relatively just or least unjust, or to the question of whether they are affected by the inadequacy of these structures. According to Paul, Christians are compelled to live "in the world" (1 Cor. 5:10), and at the same time they are told to withdraw spiritually from the world and not to be "yoked" together with unbelievers (2 Cor. 6:14). . . .

Christians can share guilt in social injustice without actually realizing it, whether because of pure ignorance (cf. G. B. Shaw's play *Mrs. Warren's*

*Profession*) or because of an education that holds certain class privileges to be right which objectively are not so considering society as a whole. In such circumstances, the Church—both clergy and laity—has the duty to sensitize public opinion and thus usher in a more just balance of goods, without, for all that, globally condemning as "sinful" such a highly complex economic system as "capitalism."

Today more than ever competent Christians should become active in the social, economic and political sectors of society, where one necessarily confronts hard contradictions and struggles, and where compromise always represents the best solution ("Politics is the art of the possible"). The evangelical "peacemaker" has to set up shop precisely between parties in conflict, between employers and employees, political factions and economic groups. Only by the—dramatic!—collaboration of all will the structures be "converted" from their "sinfulness" and change more effectively than by violent overthrows or brutal nationalizations behind which there are very often goals sought in utopian and unrealistic fashion.

The urgency of the practical concerns of liberation theology is not called into question by any criticism that may be made of it. But the totality of God's revelation to the world can in no way be reduced to political and social liberation, nor even to the general concept of liberation. Liberation theology has its specific place in a theology of the Kingdom of God. It is *one* aspect of the whole of theology and, in practical terms, it demands the Church's commitment to the shaping of the world as a whole in a manner conforming with Christ.

*Jon Sobrino, SJ, "The Kingdom of God and the Theological Dimension of the Poor," in* Who Do You Say That I Am? *ed. John C. Cavadini and Laura Holt (Notre Dame, IN: University of Notre Dame Press, 2004), 113–14, 115–16, 120, 122, 124, 126, 128, 137–38*

Forgetting the poor has gone hand in hand with forgetting the Kingdom of God. The latter is something that occurred gradually in Christology. Christology, in effect, developed from two starting points: the experience of Jesus' *resurrection* and the recollection of his *historical life*. Now, as far as his life goes, according to the synoptic gospels, Jesus' existence unfolded in an essential twofold relation: to God who is *Abba* and to the *Kingdom* of God. However already in an incipient way in the New Testament, and certainly subsequent to it, *Christology*—the resurrection now a given—was developed in a fairly exclusive way from the starting point of the relationship that Jesus had with God—*Abba*. The result was that within a period of ten to twenty years (according to Martin Hengel) Christology had taken up the orientation that it has followed to this very day: *Jesus is the Son of God*. Jesus' relation to the Kingdom of God, equally constitutive during his lifetime, gradually disappeared from christological thought, or, more precisely, was reinterpreted in such a way that with the passage of time its original content was ignored, as well as its centrality and its capacity to articulate the reality of salvation. By the time of the fourth-century conciliar debates it is clear that the Kingdom of God plays no role whatsoever in Christology.

In other words, faith in Christ rendered itself theoretical by relating itself to the *person of God* (which is better expressed in the titles of Son, Lord, Word—those titles that were most frequently used in the christological councils) and not—in addition—to the *Kingdom of God*. Jesus' most intimate reality came to be seen in terms of *filiation*, sacrament of the Father, historical presence of God in this world, and this (which is good news, to be sure) to the greatest degree possible in history. But the consequence of this was that even though he is also called Christ (Messiah), the title ceased to express the fact that "Messiah" was the referent of the hope and the salvation of the poor—that which points toward the Kingdom of God. It was being turned into a proper name, in practice, moreover, a merely denotative name. In this sense I have written that the Messiah was quickly "de-Messianized." Christology will go on to delve more deeply into the relation of Jesus to the Father, the reality of the Son, while progressively weakening the relation of Jesus to the Kingdom to the point of ignoring it. . . .

. . . What is central to all of the New Testament is the fact that God's plan is found not only in the appearance of Jesus, the Son, which is a genuine *eu-angelion* [*good news*], to be sure, but also in the "horizontalization," as it were, of this good news, in such a way that in relation to the Son or because of the Son this good news, which he is, overflows out toward human beings. This is why I talk about "equivalents" of the Kingdom of God, since in every stratum of the New Testament central elements of the Kingdom are captured, with varying nuances: a good news that saves the human being, first and foremost the weak; the gratuity of this salvation; its collective, social dimension; its dialectical dimension insofar as it appears in the presence of and in conflict with the forces of evil, both personal (hubris, desire, concupiscence, ambition) and "structural" (the sin of the world, principalities and powers, evil, death). . . .

The equivalents have their own dynamisms, which, even without intending it or being aware of it, can lead to the Kingdom, as Jesus proclaimed it, losing its centrality and along with that, some of its fundamental elements. In this sense I think that dynamisms unfold in the New Testament that, while carrying important values, some of which were expressed more profoundly than in the synoptic gospels (justification by faith in Paul, the capacity of love to enfold the divine and the human in John), also end up overshadowing Jesuanic values, above all those that center on the Kingdom of God. Specifically—and this is what is at issue—the centrality and privilege of the poor in God's eyes.

This overshadowing happened not long after the New Testament, and frequently without the counterweight of the magnificent theologies and the Kingdom-equivalents in Paul and John. There were cultural reasons (entry into the Graeco-Roman world, which was a culture without a utopian, hopeful, horizon), as well as social ones (the insignificance of the first communities in an empire that thought itself to be reformable but everlasting). But the fundamental reasons seem to be of the historical-theological order: Jesus' resurrection and the imminent expectation of the parousia. Both of these made it difficult to formulate the Christian utopia as the Kingdom of God. . . .

Talking about the Kingdom of God is not . . . only a matter of reclaiming "the historical Jesus"—as supremely important as this is—or only of retrieving "the historical Jesus who preached the Kingdom," but of restoring "the poor" to whom Jesus preached the Kingdom. For this reason, since the tradition of the Kingdom of God restores the poor better than other New Testament traditions and other theologies past and present—and without the dangers that the latter bring—and since it better expresses their privilege in God's eyes, we need to get back to that tradition. . . .

. . . An intimate relationship exists between the Kingdom of God and the poor. Minimally, it has to be said that Jesus announces the Kingdom to the poor because they are poor. This minimum—which is a maximum—is what has to be continually asserted. . . .

In the first place, in the synoptic gospels the poor are those who are stooped over, held in contempt, insignificant. They are characterized in a twofold way. On the one hand, the poor are those who are groaning under some kind of basic and vital need that makes survival very difficult. The most adequate metaphor is that of the *anawim*, the ones bent over under some heavy burden. On the other hand, the poor are those held in contempt by their society, "those whose religious ignorance or moral conduct, according to the conviction of the age, closed the door to salvation" [Joachim Jeremias, *New Testament Theology*, vol. 1 (New York: Charles Scribner's Sons; London: SCM Press, 1971), 112]. . . .

In the second place, in the synoptic gospels, *the poor are the majorities, the crowds, the people*. . . .

Focusing just on the people who followed Jesus, the most frequent term to describe them is *ochlos*, which designates *the crowds of people, the throng*. Their situation was extremely hard, and many times desperate; they suffered from sickness and demonic possession; they went around like sheep without a shepherd. . . .

If God privileges the poor because they are poor, then God is partial and merciful.

Dealing first with partiality, in the founding event of the faith God reveals God's self to an oppressed people because they are oppressed. It is not that God first reveals God's self to everyone and then shows partiality for the oppressed. Rather, it is in and through partiality toward them that God reveals God's proper reality. . . .

Jesus' mercy . . . is a re-action—an action, therefore—to the pain of the poor and victims, from which it is possible to define what is humanly and divinely ultimate. This is how Jesus himself is described and this is how, in Luke's gospel, he describes the upright person, the Samaritan, who is "moved with pity" (Lk 10:33—and it is certainly clear that the poor fellow here is a victim), and God himself, the Father of the Prodigal Son, who is "filled with compassion" (Lk 15:20). And finally, it is what Jesus requires of everyone: "Be merciful, just as your Father is merciful" (Lk 6:36). . . .

The poor are there before the Jesuanic martyrs. They are the ones who suffer the slow death of poverty; and they are the ones who are often assassinated violently, collectively, and with great cruelty. They are the ones that I call crucified peoples, the suffering servant of Yahweh. They go to their deaths less freely, compared with the Jesuanic martyrs, because sometimes they have no chance at all to escape. Neither do they exercise any violence, not even the violence of a prophetic word, like Archbishop Romero's. But, on the other hand, the sin of the world weighs down on them more cruelly and they are assassinated more defenselessly.

These crucified peoples ought to be an absolutely central theme for theology, although they do not even have a name any more. But, what is more, they are the ones, briefly put, who shed light on the "why" of the Jesuanic martyrs and on the martyr Jesus. The latter have been killed for defending these crucified peoples from the slow death of poverty and the violent death of repression.

## 4.2 Feminist Christologies

*Rosemary Radford Ruether, "The Liberation of Christology from Patriarchy,"*
Religion and Intellectual Life 2 (1985): 116–19

Christology should be the most comprehensive symbol of redemption from all sin and evil in . . . Christian theology, the symbol that embraces the authentic humanity and fulfilled hopes of all persons. The theological categories adopted by early Christianity to define Christology would seem to be inclusive of women. And yet it has been the Christian symbol most frequently used to exclude women from full participation in the Christian Church. How is this possible?

Early Christianity used the word "logos" to define that presence of God which has become incarnate in Jesus Christ. This term drew on a long tradition of religious philosophy. In Greek and Hellenistic Jewish philosophy, the divine Logos was the means by which the transcendent God came forth in the beginning to create the world. The Logos was simultaneously the immanence of God and the ground of creation. Through the Logos God created the world, guided it, was revealed to it and reconciled the world to God.

The Logos was particularly related to the rational principle in each human soul. By linking the term Christ, the Messiah, through which God redeemed the world, to the Logos, early Christianity prevented a split between creation and redemption threatened by early gnosticism. The God revealed in Christ was the same God who created the world in the beginning, the authentic ground of creation manifest in fulfilled form over against the alienation of creation from its true being. The term Logos as the divine identity for Christ should have been a term that pointed all humans to the foundations of their true humanity.

Yet the Greek and Hellenistic Jewish tradition was shaped in a patriarchal culture which gave the terms Logos and Christ an androcentric bias. Since rationality was presumed by these patriarchal cultures to be normatively male, all the theological reference points for defining Christ were defined androcentrically. Essential humanity, the image of God in humanity and the Logos of God were interrelated in androcentric definitions. These definitions reinforced the assumption that God was male and that Christ must therefore be male in order to reveal the male God.

Although Christianity has never said that God was literally a male, it has assumed that God represents preeminently the qualities of rationality and sovereignty. Since men are presumed to have these qualities and women not to have them, the male metaphor has been seen as appropriate for God, while female metaphors have been regarded as inappropriate. The Logos or Word which reveals the "Father" therefore also has been presumed to be properly imaged as a male. The title "Son of God", an inadequate metaphor for divine immanence, imagined as something like a parent begetting an offspring, has also been taken literally and seen as further indication that the Logos is male. These notions of the maleness of God, in turn, affected the Christian interpretation of the *imago dei*.

Genesis 1:27–28 says, "So God created man in his own image; in the image of God he created him; male and female he created them." This passage leaves open the possibility that the term man (Adam) is to be understood generically and that Genesis 1:27b teaches that this image of God is possessed equally by both sexes (which would also mean that women share in the sovereignty of "man" over the earth referred to in Genesis 1:26). But practically the whole patristic and medieval tradition rejected the possibility that women were equally theomorphic. It split the concept of *imago dei* from gender difference. This might also suggest that the *imago dei* was asexual or spiritual and therefore was neither male nor female. Gregory of Nyssa reads the text this way. But most of the Church Fathers concluded that it was the male who possessed the image of God normatively, whereas women in themselves did not possess the image of God, but rather were the image of the body, or the lower creation, which man was given to rule over. . . .

These notions of the maleness of God, the Logos, the *imago dei* and of Christ threaten to undermine the basic Christian faith that Christ indeed possesses a humanity which includes the humanity of women and that women are included in the incarnation and redemption of Christ. The Church Fathers assumed that she was included in redemption while, at the same time, being non-normative and non-theomorphic. This assumption was based on the patriarchal ideology that women lack equally human capacities for intelligence and leadership and that female humanity is included within the lower part of male humanity, ruled over by male rationality. As these assumptions are refuted by the actual incorporation of women into higher education and public leadership today, and Aristotelian biology is shown to be false, all the androcentric bases of this theological construct are thrown in question. Today a Christology which elevates Jesus' maleness to ontologically necessary significance suggests that Jesus' humanity does not represent women at all. Incarnation solely into the male sex does not include women and so women are not redeemed. That is to say, if women cannot represent Christ, then Christ does not represent women. Or, as the women's ordination movement has put it, "either ordain women or stop baptizing them". Some women believe that women should leave Christianity and seek another religion which genuinely includes their humanity in its theology of the divine-human relationship.

*Elizabeth A. Johnson, "The Maleness of Christ," in* The Power of Naming, *ed. Elisabeth Schüssler Fiorenza (Maryknoll, NY: Orbis Books; London: SCM Press, 1996), 307–8, 311–12*

The story of Jesus of Nazareth, crucified and risen, confessed as the Christ, is at the center of Christian faith in God. In the gracious power of Sophia-Spirit unleashed through his history and destiny, the community of disciples continuously retells and enacts that story as the story of God with us to heal, redeem and liberate all people and the cosmos itself. Good news indeed. But that good news is stifled when Jesus' maleness, which belongs to his historical identity, is interpreted as being essential to his redeeming christic function and identity. Then the Christ functions as a religious tool for marginalizing and excluding women. Let us be very clear: the fact that Jesus of Nazareth was a male human being is not in question. His sex was a constitutive element of his historical person along with other particularities such as his Jewish racial identity, his location in the world of first-century Galilee, and so on, and as such is to be respected. The difficulty arises, rather, from the way Jesus' maleness is construed in official and androcentric theology and ecclesial praxis. . . .

Feminist theological analysis lays bare at least three ways in which such distorted interpretation occurs.

1. Since the man Jesus is confessed to be the revelation of God, the Christ symbol points to maleness as an essential characteristic of divine being itself. This is exacerbated by exclusive use of father and son metaphors to interpret Jesus' relationship to God, and by use of the *logos*, connected in Greek philosophy with the male principle, to articulate his personal reality as God with us. "Who has seen me has seen the Father" (John 14:9). This is taken literally to mean that the man Jesus is the incarnation of the male Logos and revealer of a male Father-God, despite the evidence in scripture and tradition that the mystery of God transcends all naming and creates female reality in the divine image and likeness.

2. The belief that the Word became flesh and dwelt among us as a male indicates that thanks to their natural bodily resemblance, men enjoy a closer identification with Christ than do women. Men are not only theomorphic but, by virtue of their sex, also christomorphic in a way that goes

beyond what is possible for women. Thus men alone among human beings are able to represent Christ fully. While women may be recipients of divine grace, they are unsuited to carry out christic actions publicly because of their sexual difference from his maleness. For this mentality, the idea that the Word might have become female flesh is not even seriously imaginable, so incapable of christic identity are women thought to be; and this, despite the doctrine of creation and the church's praxis and theology of baptism.

3. Given the dualism which essentially divorces male from female humanity, the maleness of Christ puts the salvation of women in jeopardy. The Christian story of salvation involves not only God's compassionate will to save but also the method by which that will is effective, namely, by plunging into sinful human history and transforming it from within. The early Christian aphorism, "What is not assumed is not healed," sums up the insight that God's saving solidarity with humanity is what is crucial for the birth of the new creation. As the Nicene Creed confesses, "*et homo factus est*" ("and was made man"). But if in fact what is meant is *et vir factus est*, if maleness is essential for the christic role, then women are cut out of the loop of salvation, for female sexuality was not assumed by the Word made flesh. [*In Latin*, vir *can only be used of a male person*, homo *of both female and male*.] Thus, to Rosemary Radford Ruether's searching question, "Can a male saviour save women?" interpretation of the maleness of Christ as essential can only answer "No," despite Christian belief in the universality of God's saving intent (*Sexism and God-Talk: Toward a Feminist Theology*, Boston and London, Beacon, 1983, pp. 116–38). . . .

Feminist hermeneutics has blazed a trail showing how the gospel story of Jesus resists being used to justify patriarchal dominance in any form. His preaching and life-style lived and breathed the opposite, creating a challenge which brought down on his head the wrath of religious and civil authority. They crucified him. In the light of this history Jesus' maleness can be seen to have a definite social significance. If a woman had preached compassionate love and enacted a style of authority that serves, she would have been greeted with a colossal shrug. Is this not what women are supposed to do by nature? But from a social position of male privilege Jesus preached and acted this way, and herein lies the summons. The cross, too, is a sturdy symbol of the "kenosis of patriarchy," the self-emptying of male dominating power in favour of the new humanity of compassionate service and mutual empowerment. The Gospel story of Jesus makes it clear that the heart of the problem is not that Jesus was male, but that more males have not been like Jesus.

What then of Christ? Clues for feminist interpretation can be found in the resurrection, wisdom christology, and the biblical symbol of the body of Christ.

The resurrection is a mystery of faith enveloped in the mystery of God. It negates a simple literalism that imagines Jesus still existing as in the days of his earthly life, only now invisible. Jesus has truly died, with all that this implies of change: he is gone from the midst of history according to the flesh. Faith in the resurrection affirms that God has the last word for this executed victim of state injustice and that word, blessedly, is life. Jesus with all his historicity is raised into glory by the power of the Spirit. What this ringing affirmation precisely means is inconceivable. His life is now hidden in the holy mystery of God, while his presence is known only through the Spirit wherever two or three gather, bread is broken, the hungry fed. But this indicates a transformation of his humanity so profound that it escapes our imagination. The humility of the apophatic approach acknowledges that language about the maleness of Christ at this point proceeds under the negating sign of analogy, more dissimilar than similar to any maleness known in history.

New Testament wisdom christology construes Christ Jesus in terms of the powerful female figure of Sophia who is creator, redeemer and divine renewer of the people of Israel, and indeed of the whole earth (Wisdom 7:10). Speaking her words, doing her deeds, and encountering her rejection, Jesus is depicted as the child of Sophia, her prophet, and ultimately even her incarnation (Luke 11:49 and Matt. 23:34; John 1). It is this identification which links the crucified prophet to the very creation of the world, and sets the church's feet on the road to Nicaea. The christology of Jesus Sophia shatters the male dominance carried in exclusive language about Jesus as the eternal male Logos or Son of the Father, enabling articulation of even a high incarnational christology in strong and gracious female metaphors.

*Sarah Coakley, "Kenōsis and Subversion," in* Swallowing a Fishbone,
*ed. Daphne Hampson (London: SPCK, 1996), 82–83, 107–10*

In an important passage in *Theology and Feminism*, Daphne Hampson tackles the question of christological *kenōsis*, or "voluntary self-emptying on the part of the second person of the Trinity". Citing Rosemary Radford Ruether's view that Jesus' self-emptying offers a challenge to patriarchy, she counters with the thought that "it is far from clear that the theme of *kenōsis* is the way in which monotheism would need to be qualified in order to bring the understanding of God more into line with feminist values". She goes on:

> That it [*kenōsis*] should have featured prominently in Christian thought is perhaps an indication of the fact that men have understood what the male problem, in thinking in terms of hierarchy and domination, has been. It may well be a model which men need to appropriate and which may helpfully be built into the male understanding of God. *But . . . for women, the theme of self-emptying and self-abnegation is far from helpful as a paradigm.* (*Theology and Feminism*, Oxford, Blackwell, 1990, p. 155; *my emphasis*)

What are we to make of Hampson's rejection of *kenōsis* and Ruether's equally staunch—though brief—defence of it? The matter clearly cuts close to the heart of what separates Christian and post-Christian feminism; and hence my focus on it in this volume. Here, in *kenōsis*, it seems, is a Christic "bone" on which Hampson chokes; for her, female "autonomy" is a supreme good which Christology can only undermine, not enhance. In contrast, for me, what rightly distinguishes Christian feminism from various secular versions of it must necessarily lie in this disputed christological realm: here, if anywhere, Christian feminism has something corrective to offer secular feminism.

It will be the burden of this essay, then, to offer a defence of some version of *kenōsis* as not only compatible with feminism, but vital to a distinctively Christian manifestation of it, a manifestation which does not eschew, but embraces, the spiritual paradoxes of "losing one's life in order to save it". . . .

What I have elsewhere called the "paradox of power and vulnerability" is I believe uniquely focused in this act of silent waiting on the divine in prayer. This is because we can only be properly "empowered" here if we cease to set the agenda, if we "make space" for God to be God. Prayer which makes this "space" may take a variety of forms, and should not be conceived in an élitist way; indeed, the debarring of "ordinary" Christians from "contemplation" has been one of the most sophisticated—and spiritually mischievous—ways of keeping lay women (and men) from exercising religious influence in the western church. Such prayer may use a repeated phrase to ward off distractions, or be wholly silent; it may be simple Quaker attentiveness, or take a charismatic expression (such as the use of quiet rhythmic "tongues"). What is sure, however, is that engaging in any such regular and repeated "waiting on the divine" will involve great personal commitment and great personal risk; to put it in psychological terms, the dangers of a too-sudden uprush of material from the unconscious, too immediate a contact of the thus-disarmed self with God, are not inconsiderable. To this extent the careful driving of wedges—which began to appear in the western church from the twelfth century on—between "meditation" (discursive reflection on Scripture) and "contemplation" (this more vulnerable activity of "space-making"), were not all cynical in their attempts to keep contemplation "special". But whilst risky, this practice is profoundly transformative, "empowering" in a mysterious "Christic" sense; for it is a feature of the *special* "self-effacement" of this gentle space-making—this yielding to divine power which is no worldly power—that it marks one's willed engagement in the pattern of cross and resurrection, one's deeper rooting and grafting into the "body of Christ". "Have *this* mind in you", wrote Paul, "which was also in Christ Jesus"; the meaning of that elliptical phrase in Greek still remains obscure, but I am far from being the first to interpret it in this spiritual sense, as a "hidden self-emptying of the heart".

If, then, these traditions of Christian "contemplation" are to be trusted, this rather special form of "vulnerability" is not an invitation to be battered; nor is its silence a silenc*ing*. (If anything, it builds one in the courage to give prophetic voice.) By choosing to "make space" in this way, one "practises" the "presence of God"—the subtle but enabling presence of a God who neither shouts nor forces, let alone "obliterates". No one can *make* one "contemplate" (though the grace of God invites it); but it is the simplest thing in the world *not* to "contemplate", to turn away from that grace. Thus the "vulnerability" that is its human condition is not about asking for unnecessary and unjust suffering (though increased self-knowledge can indeed be painful); nor is it (in Hampson's words) a "self-abnegation". On the contrary, this special "self-emptying" is not a negation of self, but the place of the self's transformation and expansion into God. . . .

Where, then, finally, does gender find its place in the "contemplative" reception to the divine I have tried to describe? The answer is in one sense obvious: is not such willed "passivity" a traditionally "female" trait? Is not this precisely why "mystical" literature has so greatly emphasized the huge psychic reversals for men engaged in such "submission" to the divine? And hence, is not the obvious danger here the one with which we started, that is Hampson's charge that *kenōsis* may only be "useful" to men, as a complement to their masculinism? But I have already tried to hint at a way in which I believe the contemplative exercise may take us beyond such existing gender stereotypes, up-ending them in its gradual undermining of *all* previous certainties and dogmatisms. Here, if I am right, is "power-in-vulnerability", the willed effacement to a gentle omnipotence which, far from "complementing" masculinism, acts as its undoing. And whilst spiritual *kenōsis*, thus construed, may, in our current cultural climate, be easy for men to avoid altogether, and even easier, perhaps, for women seriously to misconstrue (as "appropriate" sexual submission), we cannot rest while such implied "essentialist" visions of gender still exercise us. When Hampson talks of the "male" God I fear she is thus resting.

### 4.3 Black and Asian Christologies

*Jacquelyn Grant, "Subjectification as a Requirement for Christological Construction," in* Lift Every Voice, *rev. and exp., ed. Susan Brooks Thistlethwaite and Mary Potter Engel (Maryknoll, NY: Orbis Books, 1998), 210–11, 215–16.*

Who do Black People say that Jesus Christ Is?

It is the thesis of Black theologians that christology is constructed from the interplay of social context, scripture, and traditions. The significance of social context is addressed in the first chapter of James Cone's book, *God of the Oppressed* [New York: Seabury Press, 1975]. Cone crystallizes the issue in the following way: "The focus on social context means that we cannot separate our questions about Jesus from the concreteness of everyday life. We ask, 'Who is Jesus Christ for us today?' because we believe that the story of his life and death is the answer to the human story of oppression and suffering" [108–9].

The social context for Black christology is the Black experience of oppression and the struggle against it. Christology is irrelevant if it does not take this into account, because historically christology has been constructed in the context of white superiority, ideology, and domination. Christ has functioned to legitimate these social and political realities. Essentially, Christ has been white. For "white conservatives and liberals alike . . . Christ is a mild, easygoing white American who can afford to mouth the luxuries of 'love,' 'mercy,' 'long-suffering,' and other white irrelevances, because he has a multibillion dollar military force to protect him from the encroachment of the ghetto and the 'communist conspiracy'" [James H. Cone, *A Black Theology of Liberation* (Philadelphia: Lippincott, 1970), 198].

To counteract this historical and theological trend, what the late Bishop Joseph Johnson called "the tragedy of the white Christ," Black theologians have called not only for a new departure in theology but more specifically for a new christological interpretation. This white Christ must be eliminated from the Black experience and the concept of a Black Christ must emerge.

The claims for the blackness of Christ are argued by Black theologians in several different ways. Albert Cleage's position leaves no room for guessing his meaning. Postulating actual historical Blackness, Cleage argues that Jesus was a Black Jew. From Cleage's perspective it is simply impossible to believe that Jesus could have been anything but Black, given the established fact of "the intermingling of races in Africa and the Mediterranean area" [Albert Cleage, *The Black Messiah* (New York: Sheed & Ward, 1968), 3]. James Cone . . . finds that Blackness clarifies the incarnation in its specificity. Wilmore finds the meaning of "the Black Messiah" to be "the relevance of the Person and the Work of Christ for existence under the condition of oppression" [Gayraud Wilmore, "The Black Messiah," *Journal of the Interdenominational Theological Center* 2 (1974): 13–14]. Rejected, despised, and acquainted with grief—both biblically and on the contemporary scene—this is the christological symbol: God loves the outcast. . . .

## Who Do Womanists say that Jesus Christ Is?

Black women have said and continue to say that Jesus Christ is one of us. When we see Jesus Christ, we see both the particular Jesus of Nazareth and the universal Christ of faith. In Jesus Christ, we see an oppressed experience and at the same time we see liberation. When we see Jesus Christ, we see concreteness and absoluteness, for in Jesus Christ, the absolute becomes concrete.

Black women can identify with this Jesus Christ because the Jesus Christ reality is so akin to their own reality. For it is in the context of Black women's experience that we find the particular connecting with the universal. By this I mean that in each of the three dynamics of oppression which characterize their reality, Black women share in the reality of a broader community: they share race suffering with Black men; with white women and other Third World women they are victims of sexism; and with poor Blacks and whites, and other Third World peoples, especially women, they are disproportionately poor. To speak of Black women's tridimensional reality, therefore, is not to speak of Black women exclusively, for there is an implied universality which connects them with others.

Similarly, there was an implied universality with Jesus Christ, which made him identify with others—the poor, the women, the stranger. To affirm Jesus' solidarity with the "least of the people" (Matt: 25:31–46) is not an exercise in romanticized contentment with one's oppressed status in life. For the resurrection signified that there is more to the life of Jesus Christ than the cross. For Black women, the resurrection signifies that their triply oppressive existence is not the end. It represents the context in which a particular people struggle to experience hope and liberation. Jesus Christ thus represents a threefold significance: first, he identifies with the "little people"—Black women—where they are and he accompanies them in their struggles. Second, he affirms the basic humanity of these, "the least," and in affirming them he empowers them to gain "more." Third, he inspires active hope in the struggle for resurrected, liberated existence. Christ's empowerment effects liberation.

*Mercy Amba Oduyoye, "Jesus Christ," in* The Cambridge Companion to Feminist Theology, *ed. Susan Frank Parsons (Cambridge: Cambridge University Press, 2002), 152, 165–67*

In dealing with Christologies in Africa, one finds two major trends, the inculturationalist and the liberationist. The first type are those who consciously appropriate Africa's traditional experience of God. We note that the Greek Bible imagery that forms the foundations of traditional Christologies has appropriated beliefs and language from Jewish religion, as well as Graeco-Roman paradigms. To talk intelligently about new experience, one cannot but build upon what is known. African religion and culture furnish the language of Christologies that describe Jesus as an ancestor, a king or elder brother. These carry notions of mediatorship and authority. It is as an ancestor that Jesus stands between humanity and God as the spokesperson, as the *Okyeame*; Jesus is interpreter and advocate. We name ourselves Christians after his being the Christ, just as we name our children after our worthy forebears.

We say Christ is king and we see the lives of royal leaders who were compassionate and brave community builders. We see the royal leaders of the Akan, who bear the title *Osagyefo*, the one who saves the battle, the victorious warrior, and we see Jesus as *Nana*, both ancestor and royalty. In several African traditional cultures, the rulers are regarded as hedged by divinity, and so one is able to talk about the Christ being both divine and human without raising the philosophical debates of early Christianity. So praying to and through Jesus follows naturally and is practised as the spirituality of the religion that enables Christians to face the daily realities of life.

Women had employed cultural paradigms to describe their belief in Jesus, but those that are most favoured are the cultural ones that are also liberative. They employ myths of wonder-workers who save their communities from hunger and from the onslaught of their enemies, both physical and spiritual. The women's Christology in large measure therefore falls within the category of the liberationist types. Jesus is the brother or kin who frees women from the domination of inhuman husbands. They relate more easily to the Christ who knew hunger, thirst, and homelessness, and see Jesus as oppressed by the culture of his own people. Jesus the liberator is a paradigm for the critique of culture that most African women theologians do. . . .

My reading of African women's theology is that they have had no problem of particularising the "Christ of God" in the man of Nazareth. They know of saviours in their own histories; some are men, others are women. Their stance is that the maleness of Jesus is unjustly capitalised on by those who want to exclude women, but that does not detract from the fact that in Jesus' own practice, inclusion is the norm. What Edet says about the humanity of Jesus was that it is the humanity of woman, and African women should and do claim Jesus as their liberator. They claim the soundly constructed so-called feminine traits they find in Jesus—his care and compassion for the weak and excluded. The anti-hunger ministry, healing, and the place of children in his words and works—all go together to create a bonding around women's lives that African women feel with Jesus. He is one of us, knows our world, and can therefore accompany us in our daily joys and struggles.

What alienates some African women is the interpretation of revelation that suggests that before Jesus Africans had not encountered God and that without Jesus all are doomed. The Christian exclusiveness is in large measure not biblical and is therefore not allowed to become an obstacle in the multireligious communities of Africa. African women theologians have often reinterpreted the exclusiveness of John as a directive to walk in the path of Jesus. Elizabeth Amoah would say, "Jesus is the only way" is a call to the recognition that to make salvation a reality for all, we all should walk in the way of Jesus and live the truth of the implication of a kenotic life. . . .

The victory of Jesus is not over other nations and cultures. It is over death and life-denying forces. . . .

The Christ of the women of Africa upholds not only motherhood, but all who like Jesus of Nazareth perform "mothering roles" of bringing out the best in all around them. The present profit-centred economies of our world deny responsibly to bring life to the dying and to empower those challenged by the multitude of impairments that many have to live with. Justine Kahungu Mbwiti, in a study of Jesus and a Samaritan woman (John 4:1–42), draws out several of the images of Jesus that empower African women [J. K. Mbwiti, "Jesus and the Samaritan Woman," in *Talitha Qumi! Proceedings of the Convocation of African Women Theologians*, ed. M. A. Oduyoye and M. R. A. Kanyoro (Ibadan: Daystar, 1989 and 1990), 63–76]. As rural women, they see the scandal of the incarnation, the appearance of God in the hinterlands of the Roman Empire as God coming to their rural and slum situations. They relate to Jesus who deliberately shakes what was customary as a sign of renewal that opens for them the space to put critical questions to what was traditional. They referred to the scandalous action in the temple (John 2:13–16), and the many violations of the Sabbath (John 5:1–18), as affirmation that life is to be lived consciously and conscientiously. Jesus becomes therefore not just the one by whom God saves; He is Himself the Saviour.

*Monica J. Melanchthon, "Christologies, Asian," in* The SCM Dictionary of Third World Theologies, *ed. Virginia Fabella, MM, and R. S. Sugirtharajah (London: SCM Press, 2003), 47–50*

## Inculturation Christologies

Indian Hindus who focused on the nature of the person of Jesus Christ did many of the early christological reflections in Asia. While their articulations reveal a genuine fondness and awe for Jesus, their attempts disclose loyalty to the tradition to which they belonged since they drew only upon images from the Hindu philosophical systems that they hoped would bridge the gap between the two faiths. The result was a mystical and metaphysical interpretation of the person and work of Christ. . . .

The efforts of these pioneers inspired several Indian Christians to develop christological articulations rooted in the Indian culture. Hence Jesus has been identified as *logos* or *cit*, or consciousness, but fully human and fully divine (Brahmobandhav Upadhyaya); as *prajapati* or Lord of the created world (K. M. Banerjee); as incarnation or *avatara* (Sadhu Sundar Singh and V. Chakkarai); as the *antaryamin* or the immanent Christ (A. J. Appasamy); as Adi Purusha or the historic figure permanently human (P. Chenchiah); and as the eternal *Om* or *logos* (S. Jesudasan). A later development in Asian Christian theology, particularly in India, saw an emphasis on humanization and liberation of people in the social and political realm. Much of this was done within the context of rising nationalism and the need for dialogue between religions. Jesus Christ was therefore referred to as the Hidden One (J. N. Farquhar); the Crown of Hinduism (R. Panikkar); the Acknowledged Christ (M. M. Thomas); and so on. It is well known that the roots of Indian Christian theology are found in the experiences of theologians who are mainly from the upper caste/class communities. An authentic contextual theology to them meant an adaptation or adjustment to the dominant ethos in India, which therefore included the acceptance and continuance of the caste structure. Influenced by the Hindu philosophical systems and other Hindu literature such as the Vedas and the Upanishads, their theology differed from that of the Christian masses who were poor and illiterate and belonged to the Scheduled caste groups. Their articulations of Christ did not challenge but protected the interest of the dominant castes. Christological thinking has also been informed by the distinct Indian concept of "guru" or teacher, which enables one to perceive Jesus as the revelation or presence of God in a freer manner while at the same time transforming the understanding of the term itself when Jesus' teachings and works are considered (M. Thomas Thangaraj).

## Popular Christologies

Outside the mainline theological circles are the many popular christologies, which range from the traditional to the radical: Jesus as one who bestows prosperity, the magician, the miracle man, the stiff and the stern judge, the spiritual being and world-negating God, the eschatological Christ, to name a few. The work of Jesus is understood to be that of one who has been sent to call the people to repentance and a life of adoration of God. This focus on the spiritual dimension of salvation places Jesus over the cultural conflicts of caste, religion, gender, language, and class and therefore outside the debate, so to speak. The infant Jesus is also worshipped as a symbol of protection in times of danger and hardship and as the bestower of wishes. Many Asian Christians identify with the Christ of the cross and pay little attention to resurrection. Their vision does not go beyond the satisfaction of their immediate personal needs and hence lacks a social dimension. Yet there are others for whom Christ is a model to be emulated in the struggle for liberation. "To have faith in the incarnate, crucified and resurrected Christ means to be part of his revolutionary task to liberate man" (Salvador Martinez).

## Christologies and Religious Pluralism

Challenged by religious pluralism, Asian christological thinking over the past decade has, with the realization that religious pluralism is something to be valued and not merely tolerated, embarked on the project of bringing the "person of Jesus in conjunction with other religious figures, into a revitalizing and enriching encounter with them and with Christian faith itself" (Sugirtharajah). Explorations have been made into the similarities between Jesus and other religious figures, resulting in connections being made between Jesus and Krishna and the salvation they both offer (Ovey N. Mohammed); Jesus and the Buddha as two enlightened individuals (Seiichi Yagi), both involved in the act of human liberation (Aloysius Pieris). In the light of the Chinese concept of *yin* and *yang*, Jesus has been conceived as the way of change and progress and has provided new insights into the understanding of humanity/divinity, death/resurrection, and creation/redemption (Jung Young Lee). Within the Islamic context, it has been suggested that christological affirmations need to be divested of ideas, images, and language that are offensive to the Islamic community and focused instead on the "greatness of God," as exemplified in Jesus (Alexander Malik). Others have proposed a God-centered christology that is also mystery (Stanley Samartha); or Jesus as one among the many manifestations of the Universal Word (Michael Amaladoss).

## Liberation Christologies

At present, christological reflections stand at a new crossroad. Asian theologians are attempting to articulate christologies that take into consideration the massive and acute suffering of the Asian people, the widespread poverty, injustice, ethnic, caste, racial, and religious differences, and the increasing violence that characterize Asian communities. Against this backdrop, Asian theologians have articulated christologies within a theological paradigm with a liberation stance. Hence, we have Jesus identified as "pain-love"—who embodies the pain of the Asian people through the passion of his own pain on the cross (C. S. Song); Jesus as the center moving toward those at the periphery (Kosuke Koyama); Jesus as the prophet, a subversive-creative individual (Sebastian Kappen); Jesus as the hope and the way to liberation (Michael Rodrigo); and the *minjung* Christ as one who is not the Christ of the kerygma but the historical Jesus who associates and lives with the *minjung* [people]. For the *dalits* [untouchables] in India, Christ embraces them in their suffering, rejection, and shame. Jesus, by virtue of his humanity, his roots, his solidarity with the outcastes, his total identification with the poor, his being the servant God and the suffering servant, and most of all because of his dying on the cross and exemplifying brokenness, for allowing himself to be crushed, split, and torn, by virtue of his experience of Godforsakenness is the prototype of a *dalit*. Jesus is therefore a *dalit* in the fullest sense of the term, one who belongs to the realm of the outside, the region of carcasses and defilement.

## 4.4 A Universal Christology?

*Rowan Williams*, On Christian Theology *(Oxford: Blackwell, 2000), 103–5*

Christianity cannot set out its distinctive proposal with full seriousness in the absence of some account of the "embodying" or incarnation of God in Christ; and, as I have tried to indicate, both the significance and the difficulty of speaking about this derive from the context of a particular religio-political history. It is unhelpful to treat it as a specific case of a general mythological pattern of divine embodiment, in abstraction from the call-and-response, promise-and-fulfilment grammar of Jewishness. To ask, with John Hick in a celebrated essay [in *The Myth of God Incarnate* (London: SCM Press, 1993), 176], whether Jesus might not have been conscripted into an avatar pattern [*as in the Hindu belief in multiple "incarnations"*] if the gospel had travelled as far eastwards as it did westwards is to miss the point: the "divinity" of Jesus becomes a theological possibility and eventually a theological necessity precisely because of his relation to the institutionalized religious meanings of Israel (this sets the agenda even for the developments of more obviously Hellenistic speculations such as Logos theology), and insofar as the background of Israel remained part of the story of Jesus, this story would generate its own myth and dogma, rather than simply being absorbed into another mythology.

But this is to say that belief in Christ as the definitive and critical embodiment of God in Israel's history does not allow any easy transition to speaking of Christ as the "fulfilment" of all religious traditions; in fact, it makes far more difficult the idea that Christ contains, even potentially, all systems of religious meaning, let alone that the Christian Church is the final and definitive arbiter of all true insight in these matters. The history of Jesus enacts a judgement on tribalized and self-protecting religion, on the confusion between faith and ideology; it is a history of God with us insofar as it declares that there is liberty to act, to heal and to create community "outside the gates" of religious practice that has become oppressive or exclusive—God's liberty. But that liberty becomes transforming for human beings and human communities in their readiness for dispossession, for the loss of the God who is defined as belonging to us and our interests; in passing through that dispossession, religious speech moves some little way closer to being a speech that human beings as human beings may share. To be a Christian is to claim that the Jewish story with its interruption and repristination in Jesus is the most comprehensive working-out of this moment of dispossession—a religious tradition generating its own near-negation, holding in precarious juxtaposition the faithfulness of God and the alienness and freedom of God. That is nothing if not a debatable claim. . . .

This does seem to break through, to some extent, the options of exclusivism, inclusivism and pluralism [*in relation to other religions*]. Jesus is not dehistoricized or absolutized as an icon of significance, but neither is he depicted as the teacher of one among several possible ways of salvation. He is presented as the revelation of God: as God's question, no more, no less. Being a Christian is being held to that question in such a way that the world of religious discourse in general may hear it.

*Gerald O'Collins SJ*, Christology
*(Oxford: Oxford University Press, 1995), 317–22*

A Christology of presence displays many attractive features. It ties faith in Christ firmly to the mystery of the Trinity. It provides a thread to link all the soteriological mysteries: from creation, through the incarnation (and its proximate preparation in the OT), the ministry of Jesus, his crucifixion, the resurrection, his self-bestowal in the life of the Church, the activity of the Holy Spirit within and beyond the Christian community, the role of Christ in human history and world religions, and his inauguration of the universal eschaton in which through him God will be unavoidable and publicly there for all.

This Christology of presence . . . yields at the horizontal level (between Christ and us rather than "vertically" between Christ and "Abba") a bodily vision of things. Christ is there whenever and wherever we encounter the body of creation, suffering human bodies, Jewish bodies, the ecclesial body (indwelt by the Holy Spirit), the "body" of world religions, and the historical "body" of humanity. His presence is mediated here and now in an infinite variety of ways and with varying degrees of intensity and clarity—until the consummation of all things in his eschatological body. . . .

Love is the content of salvation through Christ; his various presences form the mode.

. . . One can plead three particular advantages for the perspective of presence: its Jewishness, its feminine face, and its spiritual, pastoral, and even mystical possibilities. A central theme of OT theology is provided by the conviction that God is present to Israel and has promised to remain present no matter how unfaithful the people prove to be. The Jews marvel at the unique divine presence which they enjoy (Deut. 4:7). God's desire to be present constantly to the chosen people manifests itself concretely in the Tent of Meeting (e.g. Exod. 26; 36; 40) and then, of course, through the temple in Jerusalem. More than any other prophet Ezekiel values the divine presence symbolized by the temple, mourns the departure of God's glory (Ezek. 10:1–22; 11:22–5), and looks forward in hope to the divine presence returning when the temple is restored (Ezek. 40:1–48:35). Such key figures in the OT history as Isaac, Jacob, and Moses receive from God a special promise of presence ("I am with you") in carrying out their divinely authorized mission (e.g. Gen. 26:24; 28:15; Exod. 3:12; 4:12). The assurance of the divine presence forms a regular feature of these commissioning narratives (see also e.g. Josh. 1:5, 9; Judg. 6:12, 16; 2 Sam. 7:3). Given the persistent importance of the divine presence in OT religious thought it is not surprising that this theme emerges in Matthew, the most Jewish of the four Gospels. Recognizing that Jesus comes as the climax in the story of a people to whom God has been uniquely present (Matt. 1:1–17), Matthew calls him "Emmanuel" or "God with us" (Matt. 1:23). It is also only Matthew who appreciates that during his earthly ministry Jesus has already replaced the Jerusalem temple as the visible sign of God's presence: "greater than the temple is here" (Matt. 12:6). In his closing missionary mandate the risen Jesus promises to be always with his disciples (Matt. 28:20), a promise which parallels the promise of divine presence that regularly accompanies OT commissions. Matthew's Jewish sense of presence emerges not only when presenting the public mission to "all nations" but also when reporting Jesus' instructions for prayer within the Church: "where two or three are gathered in my name, there am I in the midst of them" (Matt. 18:20). By praying together, believers will experience the presence of Christ, "God with us." . . .

What does the Gospel record indicate about Jesus' masculine and feminine qualities? Unquestionably we come across adversarial, masculine language and characteristics. . . .

[But] alongside such masculine characteristics we can easily uncover feminine ones. Jesus receives into his presence and nurtures little children (Mark 10:13–16 parr.; see Mark 9:33–7 parr.). He is remembered as constantly cultivating the inner life through prayer (e.g. Mark 1:12–13, 35; 6:46). The struggle in Gethsemane comes across as the more surprising, since hitherto Jesus has seemed so self-assured about his mission and identity. His sayings include some that seem downright feminine or at least do not find support in male, adversarial logic: for instance, "whoever wants to save his life will lose it, but whoever loses his life for my sake and for the gospel's will save it" (Mark 8:35). "Seek and you will find; knock and the door will be opened to you" (Matt. 7:7 par.) sounds masculine and the way to win. But letting go and losing because one hopes to be saved converges with the non-violent, feminine strength-in-surrender with which Luke portrays the death of Jesus: "Father, forgive them . . . Father, into your hands I commend my spirit" (Luke 23:34, 46). A striking testimony to the untroubled, feminine delicacy of Jesus' language emerges when we recall the image of female prostitution used at times by the OT prophets to focus the disobedience of God's people. The vivid, ugly allegories of sexual infidelity developed by Ezekiel (Ezek. 16:1–63; 23:1–40) more than hint at the male insecurity and dominance of that priest-prophet. The Jesus of the Synoptic Gospels never needs to indulge in such language. On the contrary, he does not flinch from applying to himself a very homely, female image (Luke 13:34 par.). He is present like a mother hen to shelter her chickens when they run back under her wings. Like Lady Wisdom he invites his audience: "come to me, all you who labour and are heavily burdened, and I will give you rest" (Matt. 11:28). John's Gospel develops its feminine version of Jesus in various ways: for instance, through the discourse on the nurturing bread of life which evokes Lady Wisdom's banquet (John 6:22–58; Prov. 9:1–18), and the allegory of the branches that dwell in the receptive vine and bear much fruit through that welcoming presence (John 15:1–10).

A third advantage offered by a Christology of presence surfaced already in the spirituality and mysticism of the Middle Ages. Anselm, Bernard, women mystics and others fostered a tender devotion to Jesus as friend, lover, and mother. Alongside such masculine images as the warrior who paradoxically conquers evil through his death, spiritual teachers and mystics developed feminine images of a Jesus who is there to harbour and nurture those who turn to and delight in his presence. . . .

Anyone who works today in the Christian ministry knows full well what a decisive difference it makes when people enjoy a sense of Jesus' living presence. They can re-enact then the experience of the individuals portrayed in John's Gospel, who by encountering Jesus find meaning in such basic challenges as religious doubt (Nicodemus), an irregular marital situation (the Samaritan woman), and a physical handicap (the man born blind). Jesus' presence engenders meaning and creates life for them.

## Topics for Discussion

1. What significance do you attach to the term "liberation"? How does it relate to more traditional religious words such as "salvation" or "redemption," and to secular terms such as "development"?
2. In what sense should the doctrines of creation, the exodus, the cross, and the resurrection all be seen as concerned with liberation? Are they all concerned with it in the same way?
3. To what extent is it legitimate to interpret the life and teaching of Christ in social terms? What is the proper relation between the personal and the sociopolitical in Christian doctrine?
4. What are the implications of placing orthopraxis (right action) above orthodoxy? Does this make truth less important than action, and what implications does this have for one's understanding of the church?
5. How true is it that the use of male images has resulted in the God of Jesus Christ being presented as authoritarian and rationalist?
6. What kinds of correctives can feminist theology offer? Does kenosis merely reinforce female submissiveness?
7. Should appropriate images for Christ also be drawn from native African and Asian cultures, or would this distort the nature of Christianity?
8. How is the dialogue between the various world religions best envisaged? How far are translation exercises possible—that is, the use of categories from another religion as a way of explaining one's own?

# Acknowledgments

Grateful acknowledgment is given to the publishers and authors of the following works for the use of copyrighted text:

John Austin Baker, *The Foolishness of God* (London: Darton, Longman & Todd, 1970). Reprinted by permission of Darton, Longman & Todd Ltd.

Hans Urs von Balthasar, "Jesus, the Absolutely Singular," in *The von Balthasar Reader*, ed. Medard Kehl, SJ, and Werner Löser, SJ, trans. Robert J. Daly, SJ, and Fred Lawrence (Edinburgh: T. & T. Clark, 1982). Reprinted by kind permission of Continuum International Publishing Group.

Karl Barth, *Church Dogmatics*, IV/1, The Doctrine of Reconciliation, trans. G. W. Bromiley (Edinburgh: T. & T. Clark, 1974). Reprinted by kind permission of Continuum International Publishing Group.

Karl Barth, *The Humanity of God*, trans. John Newton Thomas and Thomas Wieser (London: Collins, 1961). © 1956 by Theologischer Verlag Zürich. Reprinted by permission of Westminster John Knox Press and Theologischer Verlag Zürich.

Henry Bettenson, ed., "The Creed of Nicaea," "The Nicaeno-Constantinopolitan Creed," "Gregory of Nazianzus," "*Epistolae, xvii*," "The Chalcedonian Definition," in *Documents of the Christian Church* (London: Oxford University Press, 1963). Reprinted by permission of Oxford University Press.

Rudolf Bultmann, *Jesus and the Word*, trans. L. P. Smith and E. H. Lantero (London: Collins, 1958). Reprinted with the permission of Scribner, a Division of Simon & Schuster, Inc., from *Jesus and the Word* by Rudolf Bultmann. Copyright © 1934, 1958 by Charles Scribner's Sons; copyright renewed 1962, 1986 by Charles Scribner's Sons. All rights reserved.

Andrew Chester, *Messiah and Exaltation: Jewish Messianic and Visionary Traditions and New Testament Christology* (Tübingen: Mohr Siebeck, 2007). Reprinted by permission.

S. Coakley and D. S. Pailin, eds., *The Making and Remaking of Christian Doctrine* (London: Oxford University Press, 1993). Reprinted by permission of Oxford University Press.

Sarah Coakley, "Kenōsis and Subversion," in *Swallowing a Fishbone*, ed. Daphne Hampson (London: SPCK, 1996). Reprinted by permission of SPCK.

Sarah Coakley, "What Does Chalcedon Solve and What Does It Not?" in *The Incarnation: An Interdisciplinary Symposium on the Incarnation of the Son of God*, Steven T. Davis, Daniel Kendall, SJ, and Gerald O'Collins, SJ (London: Oxford University Press, 2002). Reprinted by permission of Oxford University Press.

Don Cupitt, "The Christ of Christendom," in *The Myth of God Incarnate*, ed. John Hick (London: SCM Press, 1993). Reprinted by permission of SCM Press.

Stephen T. Davis and C. Stephen Evans, "Conclusion: The Promise of Kenosis," in *Exploring Kenotic Christology*, ed. C. Stephen Evans (Oxford: Oxford University Press, 2006). Reprinted by permission of Oxford University Press.

Jacquelyn Grant, "Subjectification as a Requirement for Christological Construction," in *Lift Every Voice*, rev. and exp., ed. Susan Brooks Thistlethwaite and Mary Potter Engel (Maryknoll, NY: Orbis Books, 1998). Reprinted by permission of Orbis Books.

Brian Hebblethwaite, "The Moral and Religious Value of the Incarnation," in *Incarnation and Myth*, ed. Michael Goulder (London: SCM Press, 1979). Reprinted by permission of SCM Press.

Van Austin Harvey, *The Historian and the Believer* (London: SCM Press, 1967). Reproduced with permission of Palgrave Macmillan.

Larry W. Hurtado, *Lord Jesus Christ* (Grand Rapids: Eerdmans, 2003). © 2003 Wm. B. Eerdmans Publishing Company, Grand Rapids, Michigan. Reprinted by permission of the publisher; all rights reserved.

Willie James Jennings, "He Became Truly Human,"*Modern Theology* 12 (1996). Reproduced with permission of Blackwell Publishing Ltd.

Elizabeth A. Johnson, "The Maleness of Christ," in *The Power of Naming*, ed. Elisabeth Schüssler Fiorenza (Maryknoll, NY: Orbis Books; London: SCM Press, 1996). Reprinted by permission of SCM Press.

Hans Küng, *On Being a Christian*, trans. Edward Quinn (London: Collins, 1977); copyright © 1976 by Doubleday, a division of Random House, Inc. Used by permission of Doubleday, a division of Random House, Inc., and HarperCollins Publishers Ltd.

Herbert McCabe, OP, *God Matters* (London: Geoffrey Chapman, 1987). Reprinted by permission of The Continuum International Publishing Group.

Monica J. Melanchthon, "Christologies, Asian," in *The SCM Dictionary of Third World Theologies*, ed. Virginia Fabella, MM, and R. S. Sugirtharajah (London: SCM Press, 2003). Reprinted by permission of SCM Press and Orbis Books.

Gerald O'Collins SJ, *Christology* (Oxford: Oxford University Press, 1995*)*. Reprinted by permission of Oxford University Press.

Gerald O'Collins, SJ, *The Easter Jesus* (London: Darton, Longman & Todd, 1980). Reprinted by permission of Darton Longman & Todd Ltd.

Mercy Amba Oduyoye, "Jesus Christ," in *The Cambridge Companion to Feminist Theology*, ed. Susan Frank Parsons (Cambridge: Cambridge University Press, 2002). Reprinted with the permission of Cambridge University Press.

David A. Pailin, "The Incarnation as a Continuing Reality," *Religious Studies* 6 (1970). Reprinted with permission of Cambridge University Press.

Wolfhart Pannenberg, *Systematic Theology*, vol. 3, trans. Geoffrey W. Bromiley (Grand Rapids: Wm. B. Eerdmans; Edinburgh: T. & T. Clark, 1998). Reprinted by kind permission of Continuum International Publishing Group.

Rosemary Radford Ruether, "The Liberation of Christology from Patriarchy," *Religion and Intellectual Life* 2 (1985). Reproduced with permission of Blackwell Publishing Ltd.

Edward Schillebeeckx, *Jesus*, trans. Hubert Hoskins (London: Collins; New York: Seabury Press, 1979). Reprinted by permission of HarperCollins Publishers Ltd. and the author. © Edward Schillebeeckx 1979.

Jon Sobrino, SJ, "The Kingdom of God and the Theological Dimension of the Poor," in *Who Do You Say That I Am?* ed. John C. Cavadini and Laura Holt (Notre Dame, IN: University of Notre Dame Press, 2004).Reprinted with permission of University of Notre Dame Press.

Robert W. Thomson, trans., Athanasius, *De Incarnatione*, in *Athanasius: Contra Gentes and De Incarnatione* (Oxford: Clarendon Press, 1971). Used by permission of Oxford University Press.

Paul Tillich, *Systematic Theology*, vol. 2 (Chicago: University of Chicago Press, 1967). Reprinted by permission of the University of Chicago Press.

Maurice Wiles, "The Incarnation," in *God Matters*, ed. Herbert McCabe, OP (London: Geoffrey Chapman, 1987). Reprinted by permission of The Continuum International Publishing Group.

Rowan Williams, *On Christian Theology* (Oxford: Blackwell, 2000). Reprinted by permission of Blackwell Publishers.

N. T. Wright, *Jesus and the Victory of God* (London: SPCK, 1996). Reprinted by permission of SPCK.

# Glossary of Christological Terms

## David Brown

**Person/*prosōpon*.** The term has a complicated history, which affects doctrine. The Greek *prosōpon* designates a "face" or "mask" (what a Greek actor carried instead of impersonating a character), character (what the actor represents), the bearer of that character (the individual who projects a particular character), and finally a bearer of self-consciousness (he who self-consciously adopts a particular projection on the world). The Latin *persona* has a similar history, except that it never meant "face" but seems to have been borrowed from the Etruscan for "mask." Though these different meanings developed over time, all continued in use in the patristic period. The last sense is the most common in our culture but historically played the least important role. The term really came to prominence in the post-Cartesian individualistic world. The prominence of other meanings had its effect in the patristic period in two main areas.

*1. Nestorius's theology.* Although his intentions were orthodox, it is hard not to accuse Nestorius of playing on the ambiguities inherent in the word *prosōpon*, much as modern successor John Robinson does in *The Human Face of God*. (Does Jesus as the face that God presents to the world mean that he is God or the nearest that God can get to a human presentation of his character without himself becoming incarnate?) Likewise, Nestorius seems to play on the two meanings—"character" and "bearer of that character": for example, "To have the *prosōpon* of God is to will what God wills, whose *prosōpon* he has," or "This is the likeness of God, to have neither purpose nor will of its own but that of him whose *prosōpon* and likeness it has."

*2. Cappadocian social analogy for Trinity.* Despite the obvious social analogies offered, like an army or marriage or three friends, their account is often denied as being really social because that is thought to imply tritheism. But

113

this is only so when we operate with the modern view of the person as an individual self-consciousness. By contrast, the older view of the person as bearer of a social identity in relation to others meant that to speak of a Trinity without reference to the social relations that constituted persons would have been seen as unintelligible. An extreme example of this attitude in Latin is the legal tag *Servus non habet personam*, "A servant does not have a legal identity as a person" (because he had no social relations, no external projection, independent of his master).

***Homoousios.*** Being "of the same substance." This term was adopted at Nicaea to describe the relation between the three persons, but it does so in spite of an earlier ambiguous history. *Homoousios* firmly excluded Arius, while another reason for acceptance of the term may have been imperial pressure, as Hosius of Cordova used it to express the Latin *consubstantialis* and Hosius was chief ecclesiastical adviser to the emperor Constantine.

Scholars disagree on what precise interpretation of *homoousios* was intended at Nicaea, as between Aristotle's first substance (individual, numeric identity—that is, "same thing") and second substance (generic identity—that is, "same kind of thing"). Kelly accepts the former, Stead the latter. Kelly thought that this interpretation was brought about by Western influence and because of this was wholeheartedly welcomed by "only a comparatively small group, consisting of the handful of Western bishops . . . and a few others" (*Early Christian Doctrines*, 4th ed. [London: A. & C. Black, 1968], 254. However, in the 5th ed. [1977] he moved his position a little bit closer to that of Stead). But Stead notes not only that the evidence for Hosius's influence is not strong, but that pre-Nicene use of *homoousios* seems almost wholly generic: "*Homoousios* guarantees very little; it can be used of things which resemble one another merely in belonging to the created order, or to the category of substance" (*Divine Substance* [Oxford: Clarendon Press, 1977], 242–66, esp. 247).

Even Athanasius, who is often regarded as a champion of numerical identity, provides no clear examples of nongeneric uses.

The debate continued after Nicaea, with Semi-Arians continuing to try and defend another term, *homoiousios* ("of like substance"), indicating a similar kind of thing, not the same kind of thing. In the Middle Ages, however, the Western church moved firmly to an understanding in terms of numerical identity.

***Hypostasis.*** "Entity" or "person." One source of considerable confusion between the church in East and West was that two words with the same roots were used to mean different things. *Hypostasis* literally means "standing under," that is, the entity that supports attributes, as literally does the Latin *substantia* (which Tertullian is largely responsible for bringing into the discussion). But while the West used *substantia* of the Trinity as a whole—"three *personae* in one *substantia*"—terminology in the East developed to speak of "three hypostases in one *ousia*." In other words, *hypostasis* had developed to mean "individual reality" or "person." The Cappadocians gained acceptance of this formula at Constantinople in 381, as well as recognition by the West that it meant the same as their own formula, but it is important to observe that before this time usage was fluid. Thus Eusebius of Caesarea, writing to his church about the Nicene Creed, glosses "consubstantial with the Father" as "not of any other *hypostasis* and *substance*, but from the Father," while even earlier, the word in the New Testament seems to mean no more than "basis" or "foundation."

# For Further Reading

## Introductory and General

Adams, M. M. *Christ and Horrors: The Coherence of Christology*. Cambridge: Cambridge University Press, 2006.

Bockmuehl, M., ed. *The Cambridge Companion to Jesus*. Cambridge: Cambridge University Press, 2001.

Cavadini, J. C., and L. Holt, eds. *Who Do You Say That I Am? Confessing the Mystery of Christ*. Notre Dame, IN: University of Notre Dame Press, 2004.

Crisp, O. D. *Divinity and Humanity: The Incarnation Reconsidered*. Cambridge: Cambridge University Press, 2007.

Cupitt, D. *The Debate about Christ*. London: SCM Press, 1979.

Davis, S. T., ed. *Encountering Jesus: A Debate on Christology*. Atlanta: John Knox Press, 1988.

Davis, S. T., D. Kendall, and G. O'Collins, eds. *The Incarnation: An Interdisciplinary Symposium on the Incarnation of the Son of God*. Oxford: Oxford University Press, 2002.

Farrer, A. "Christ Is God" and "The Silent Christ." In *Austin Farrer: The Essential Sermons*, ed. L. Houlden, 33–36, 42–44. London: SPCK, 1991.

Feenstra, R. J. "Incarnation." In *A Companion to Philosophy of Religion*, ed. P. L. Quinn and C. Taliaferro, 532–40. Oxford: Blackwell, 1999.

Ford, D. "Christology." In *The Oxford Companion to Christian Thought*, ed. A. Hastings, A. Mason, and H. Pyper, 114–18. Oxford: Oxford University Press, 2000.

———. *Self and Salvation: Being Transformed*. Cambridge: Cambridge University Press, 1999, chap. 7.

———. *Theology: A Very Short Introduction*. Oxford: Oxford University Press, 2000, 89–110.

Ford, D., and M. Higton, eds. *Jesus*. Oxford: Oxford University Press, 2002.

Forsyth, P. T. *The Person and Place of Jesus Christ*. London: Independent Press, 1946.

Frei, H. W. *The Identity of Jesus Christ: The Hermeneutical Bases of Dogmatic Theology*. Philadelphia: Fortress Press, 1975.

Gunton, C. E. *Yesterday and Today: A Study of Continuities in Christology*. London: SPCK, 1997.

Haight, R. D. *The Future of Christology*. London: Continuum, 2005.

———. *Jesus: Symbol of God*. Maryknoll, NY: Orbis Books, 1999.

Hamilton, W. *A Quest for the Post-Historical Jesus*. London: SCM Press, 1993; New York: Continuum, 1994.

Hebblethwaite, B. *The Incarnation: Collected Essays in Christology*. Cambridge: Cambridge University Press, 1987.

———. *Philosophical Theology and Christian Doctrine*. Oxford: Blackwell, 2005, chap. 4.

Herbert, R. "The God-Man." *Religious Studies* 6 (1970): 157–73.

Holmes, S. R., and A. Murray. *The Person of Christ*. London: T. & T. Clark, 2005.

Houlden, L., ed. *Jesus: The Complete Guide*. London: Continuum, 2003.

Inbody, T. L. *The Many Faces of Christology*. Nashville: Abingdon Press, 2002.

Keck, L. E. *Who Is Jesus? History in Perfect Tense*. Columbia: University of South Carolina Press, 2000.

Lowe, W. "Christ and Salvation." In *Christian Theology: An Introduction to Its Traditions and Tasks*, ed. P. C. Hodgson and R. H. King, 3rd ed., 222–48. Minneapolis: Augsburg Fortress; London: SPCK, 2008.

Macquarrie, J. *Christology Revisited*. London: SCM Press, 2003.

———. *Jesus Christ in Modern Thought*. London: SCM Press, 2003.

Marsh, C. *Christ in Practice: A Christology of Everyday Life*. London: Darton, Longman & Todd, 2006.

Marshall, B., ed. *Readings in Modern Christology*. Oxford: Blackwell, 1998.

Neville, R. C. *Symbols of Jesus: A Christology of Symbolic Engagement*. Cambridge: Cambridge University Press, 2001.

O'Collins, G., SJ. *Christology: A Biblical, Historical, and Systematic Study of Jesus*. Oxford: Oxford University Press, 1995.

———. *Jesus: A Portrait*. London: Darton, Longman & Todd, 2008.

Pelikan, J. *Jesus through the Centuries: His Place in the History of Culture*. New Haven, CT: Yale University Press, 1999.

Porter, S. E., et al., eds. *Images of Christ: Ancient and Modern*. Sheffield: Sheffield Academic Press, 1997.

Rahner, K. *Foundations of Christian Faith: An Introduction to the Idea of Christianity*. London: Darton, Longman & Todd, 1978, part 6.

Ramm, B. L. *An Evangelical Christology: Ecumenic and Historical*. Nashville: Nelson, 1985.

Rausch, T. P., SJ. *Who Is Jesus? An Introduction to Christology*. Collegeville, MN: Liturgical Press, 2003.

Sanders, E. P. "Jesus Christ." In *Dictionary of the Bible*, ed. D. N. Freedman, 701–7. Grand Rapids: Wm. B. Eerdmans, 2000.

Schwartz, H. *Christology*. Grand Rapids: Wm. B. Eerdmans, 1998.

Shuster, M., and R. Muller, eds. *Perspectives on Christology: Essays in Honor of Paul K. Jewett*. Grand Rapids: Zondervan, 1991.

Swinburne, R. *The Christian God*. Oxford: Clarendon Press, 1994, chaps. 8–10.

———. "Could God Become Man?" In *The Philosophy in Christianity*, ed. G. Vesey, 53–70. Cambridge: Cambridge University Press, 1989.

Sykes, S. W., and J. P. Clayton, eds. *Christ, Faith, and History: Cambridge Studies in Christology*. Cambridge: Cambridge University Press, 1972.

Tanner, K. "Jesus Christ." In *The Cambridge Companion to Christian Doctrine*, ed. C. E. Gunton, 245–72. Cambridge: Cambridge University Press, 1997.

Thatcher, A. *Truly a Person, Truly God: A Post-Mythical View of Jesus*. London: SPCK, 1990.

Turner, H. E. W. *Jesus the Christ*. London: Mowbrays, 1976.

Van Inwagen, P. "Incarnation and Christology." In *Routledge Encyclopedia of Philosophy*, vol. 4, ed. E. Craig, 725–32. London: Routledge, 1998.
Wiles, M. *The Remaking of Christian Doctrine*. London: SCM Press, 1974, chap. 3.

## 1. The Shape of the Debate

Bauckham, R. *God Crucified: Monotheism and Christology in the New Testament*. Carlisle, UK: Paternoster, 1998.
Borg, M. J., and N. T. Wright. *The Meaning of Jesus: Two Visions*. London: SPCK, 1999.
Bowden, J. *Jesus: The Unanswered Questions*. London: SCM Press, 1988.
Brown, R. E. *An Introduction to New Testament Christology*. New York: Paulist Press; London: Chapman, 1994.
Burridge, R. A., and G. Gould. *Jesus Now and Then*. London: SPCK; Grand Rapids: Wm. B. Eerdmans, 2004.
Casey, M. *From Jewish Prophet to Gentile God: The Origins and Development of New Testament Christology*. Cambridge: James Clarke; Louisville, KY: Westminster/John Knox Press, 1991.
Chester, A. *Messiah and Exaltation: Jewish Messianic and Visionary Traditions and New Testament Christology*. Tübingen: Mohr Siebeck, 2007.
Chilton, B., and C. A. Evans. *Studying the Historical Jesus: Evaluations of the State of Current Research*. Leiden: E. J. Brill, 1994.
Cullmann, O. *The Christology of the New Testament*. London: SCM Press, 1963.
Dunn, J. D. G. *Christology in the Making: A New Testament Inquiry into the Origins of the Doctrine of Incarnation*. London: SCM Press, 1989.
Goulder, M., ed. *Incarnation and Myth: The Debate Continued*. London: SCM Press, 1979.
Hick, J., ed. *The Myth of God Incarnate*. London: SCM Press, 1993.
Hurtado, L. W. *How on Earth Did Jesus Become a God? Historical Questions about Earliest Devotion to Jesus*. Grand Rapids: Wm. B. Eerdmans, 2005.
———. *Lord Jesus Christ: Devotion to Jesus in Earliest Christianity*. Grand Rapids: Wm. B. Eerdmans, 2003.
Kelly, J. N. D. *Early Christian Doctrines*. London: A. & C. Black, 1977.
Kreig, R. A. *Story-Shaped Christology: The Role of Narratives in Identifying Jesus Christ*. New York: Paulist Press, 1988.
Kuitert, H. M. *Jesus: The Legacy of Christianity*. London: SCM Press, 1999.
Küschel, K.-J. *Born before All Time? The Dispute over Christ's Origin*. New York: Crossroad, 1992.
Lampe, G. W. H. "Christian Theology in the Patristic Period." In *A History of Christian Doctrine*, ed. H. Cunliffe-Jones and B. Drewery, 21–180. Edinburgh: T. & T. Clark, 1978.
Lincoln, A. T., and A. Paddison, eds. *Christology and Scripture: Interdisciplinary Perspectives*. London: T. & T. Clark International, 2007.
Longenecker, R. N. *Studies in Hermeneutics, Christology, and Discipleship*. Sheffield: Sheffield Phoenix Press, 2004.
Mackey, J. P. *Jesus the Man and the Myth: A Contemporary Christology*. London: SCM Press, 1979.
Matera, F. J. *New Testament Christology*. Louisville, KY: Westminster John Knox Press, 1999.
McGrath, A. E. *Christian Theology: An Introduction*. Oxford: Blackwell, 2001, chap. 11.

————. *The Christian Theology Reader*. Oxford: Blackwell, 2001, pp. 246–325.

McIntyre, J. *The Shape of Christology: Studies in the Doctrine of the Person of Christ*. Edinburgh: T. & T. Clark, 1998.

Moule, C. F. D. *The Origin of Christology*. Cambridge: Cambridge University Press, 1977.

Norris, R. A., ed. *The Christological Controversy*. Philadelphia: Fortress Press, 1980.

Owen, H. P. "The New Testament and the Incarnation: A Study in Doctrinal Development." *Religious Studies* 8 (1972): 221–32.

Pelikan, J. *The Emergence of the Catholic Tradition (100–600)*. Chicago: University of Chicago Press, 1975, chap. 5.

Powell, M. A. *The Jesus Debate: Modern Historians Investigate the Life of Christ*. Oxford: Lion, 1998.

Rahner, K. *Theological Investigations*. Vols. 4, 6, and 9. Baltimore: Helicon Press; London: Darton, Longman & Todd, 1961–1992.

Schnackenburg, R. *Jesus in the Gospels: A Biblical Christology*. Louisville, KY: Westminster John Knox Press, 1993.

Stead, C. *Divine Substance*. Oxford: Clarendon Press, 1977.

Tuckett, C. M. *Christology and the New Testament: Jesus and His Earliest Followers*. Edinburgh: Edinburgh University Press, 2001.

## 2. Jesus of History or Christ of Faith?

Bultmann, R. *Faith and Understanding*. Philadelphia: Fortress Press, 1987.

————. *Jesus and the Word*. New York: Charles Scribner's Sons; London: Collins, 1958.

Evans, C. S. *The Historical Christ and the Jesus of Faith: The Incarnational Narrative as History*. Oxford: Clarendon Press, 1996.

Galloway, A. D. *Wolfhart Pannenberg*. London: Allen & Unwin, 1973, chap. 3.

Harvey, V. A. *The Historian and the Believer: The Morality of Historical Knowledge and Christian Belief*. London: SCM Press, 1967, chaps. 5–6.

Johnson, R. A., ed. *Rudolph Bultmann*. London: Collins, 1987.

Kasper, W. *Jesus the Christ*. London: Burns & Oates; Mahwah, NJ: Paulist Press, 1976, chap. 2.

————. *Theology and Church*. London: SCM Press, 1989.

Küng, H. *On Being a Christian*. London: Collins, 1977, 119–65, 343–462.

Lampe, G. W. H., and D. M. MacKinnon. *The Resurrection: A Dialogue Arising from Broadcasts by G. W. H. Lampe and D. M. MacKinnon*. Edited by William Purcell. London: Mowbray, 1966.

Lonergan, B. *Method in Theology*. London: Darton, Longman & Todd, 1973, 197–234.

Marxsen, W. *The Resurrection of Jesus of Nazareth*. London: SCM Press, 1970, chaps. 7–8.

Mascall, E. L. *Theology and the Gospel of Christ: An Essay in Reorientation*. London: SPCK, 1984, chap. 2.

O'Collins, G. *The Easter Jesus*. London: Darton, Longman & Todd, 1980, chaps. 3–6.

Pannenberg, W. *Jesus—God and Man*. London: SCM Press; Philadelphia: Westminster Press, 1968.

Pannenberg, W., et al., eds. *Revelation as History*. London: Sheed & Ward, 1969, chap. 4.

Richardson, A. *History, Sacred and Profane*. London: SCM Press, 1964, 125–53.

Sanders, E. P. *Jesus and Judaism*. London: SCM Press, 1985.

Schillebeeckx, E. *Jesus: An Experiment in Christology*. London: Collins; New York: Seabury Press, 1979, chap. 1.

Schleiermacher, F. *The Christian Faith*. Edinburgh: T. & T. Clark; New York: Charles Scribner's Sons, 1928, 374–424.
Stewart, R. B. *The Resurrection of Jesus: John Dominic Crossan and N. T. Wright in Dialogue*. Minneapolis: Fortress Press, 2006.
Wright, N. T. *Jesus and the Victory of God*. London: SPCK, 1996.
———. *The Resurrection of the Son of God*. London: SPCK, 2003.

## 3. The Human God?

Baker, J. A. *The Foolishness of God*. London: Darton, Longman & Todd, 1970, 283–322.
Balthasar, H. U. von. *The von Balthasar Reader*. Edited by M. Kehl and W. Löser. Edinburgh: T. & T. Clark, 1982, 127–34.
Barth, K. *Church Dogmatics*. Vol. IV/1, *The Doctrine of Reconciliation*. Translated by G. W. Bromiley. Edinburgh: T. & T. Clark, 1974.
———. *The Humanity of God*. London: Collins, 1961.
Brown, D. *The Divine Trinity*. London: Duckworth, 1985, 126–58.
Evans, C. S., ed. *Exploring Kenotic Christology: The Self-Emptying of God*. Oxford: Oxford University Press, 2006.
Goulder, M., ed. *Incarnation and Myth: The Debate Continued*. London: SCM Press, 1979.
Hick, J., ed. *The Myth of God Incarnate*. London: SCM Press, 1993.
Jennings, W. J. "He Became Truly Human." *Modern Theology* 12 (1996): 239–55.
Knox, J. *The Humanity and Divinity of Christ: A Study of Pattern in Christology*. Cambridge: Cambridge University Press, 1967.
Lonergan, B. *Method in Theology*. London: Darton, Longman & Todd, 1973, chap. 12.
Machen, J. G. *The Virgin Birth of Christ*. London: James Clarke, 1958.
Mascall, E. L. *Theology and the Gospel of Christ: An Essay in Reorientation*. London: SPCK, 1984, chap. 3.
McCabe, H., OP. "The Myth of God Incarnate" and "The Incarnation: An Exchange (with Professor Maurice Wiles)." In *God Matters*, by H. McCabe, 54–74. London: Geoffrey Chapman, 1987.
Moltmann, J. *The Crucified God: The Cross as the Foundation and Criticism of Christian Theology*. London: SCM Press, 1974, chap. 3.
———. *The Trinity and the Kingdom of God: The Doctrine of God*. London: SCM Press, 1981, 114–21.
———. *The Way of Jesus Christ*. London: SCM Press, 1990.
Morris, T. V. *The Logic of God Incarnate*. Ithaca, NY: Cornell University Press, 1986.
Pannenberg, W. *Jesus—God and Man*. London: SCM Press, 1968. chap. 3.
Quick, O. C. *Doctrines of the Creed: Their Basis in Scripture and Meaning Today*. London: Nisbet, 1938, part 2.
Robinson, J. A. T. *The Human Face of God*. London: SCM Press, 1973.
———. "Need Jesus Have Been Perfect?" In *Christ, Faith, and History: Cambridge Studies in Christology*, edited by S. W. Sykes and J. P. Clayton, 39–52. Cambridge: Cambridge University Press, 1972.

## 4. A Christ for All?

Allen, D. "Incarnation in the Gospels and in the *Bhagavad-Gita*." In *Christian Belief in a Postmodern World: The Full Wealth of Conviction*, by D. Allen, 197–211. Louisville, KY: Westminster/John Knox Press, 1989.

Anawati, G. "Isa." In *The Encyclopaedia of Islam*, vol. 4, edited by H. Gibb et al., 81–86. Leiden: E. J. Brill.

Balthasar, H. U. von. "Liberation Theology in the Light of Salvation History." In *Liberation Theology in Latin America*, ed. J. V. Schall, 131–46. San Francisco: Ignatius Press, 1982.

Berkey, R. F., and S. A. Edwards, eds. *Christology in Dialogue*. Cleveland: Pilgrim Press, 1993.

Berryman, P. *The Religious Roots of Rebellion: Christians in Central American Revolutions*. London: SCM Press, 1984, part 1.

Boff, L. *Church, Charism, and Power: Liberation Theology and the Institutional Church*. London: SCM Press,1985, 1–31.

———. *Jesus Christ Liberator: A Critical Christology of Our Time*. London: SPCK; Maryknoll, NY: Orbis Books, 1980.

Bonino, J. M. "Christologies." In *The SCM Dictionary of Third World Theologies*, edited by V. Fabella and R. S. Sugirtharajah, 41–56. London: SCM Press, 2003.

———, ed. *Faces of Jesus: Latin American Christologies*. Maryknoll, NY: Orbis Books, 1984.

Bynum, C. W. *Jesus as Mother: Studies in the Spirituality of the High Middle Ages*. Berkeley and Los Angeles: University of California Press, 1982.

Cone, J. "Who Is Jesus Christ for Us Today?" *Christianity and Crisis* 35 (1975): 81–85.

Cragg, K. *The Christ and the Faiths: Theology in Cross-Reference*. London: SPCK; Philadelphia: Westminster Press, 1986.

Farrow, D. *Ascension and Ecclesia: On the Significance of the Doctrine of the Ascension for Ecclesiology and Christian Cosmology*. Edinburgh: T. & T. Clark; Grand Rapids: Wm. B. Eerdmans, 1999.

Grant, J. *White Women's Christ and Black Women's Jesus: Feminist Christology and Womanist Response*. Atlanta: Scholars Press, 1989.

———. "Womanist Theology: Black Women's Experience as a Source for Doing Theology, with Special Reference to Christology." *Journal of the Interdenominational Theology Center* 13 (1986): 195–212.

Greene, C. J. D. *Christology in Cultural Perspective: Marking Out the Horizons*. Carlisle, UK: Paternoster; Grand Rapids: Wm. B. Eerdmans, 2003.

Gutierrez, G. *A Theology of Liberation*. London: SCM Press; Maryknoll, NY: Orbis Books, 1988, chaps. 2 and 9.

Hennelly, A. T., ed. *Liberation Theology: A Documentary History*. Maryknoll, NY: Orbis Books, 1990, nos. 7, 25, 27, 28, 45, 53.

Hick, J. *The Metaphor of God Incarnate*. Louisville, KY: Westminster/John Knox Press; London: SCM Press, 1993.

Hopkins, J. *Towards a Feminist Christology: Jesus of Nazareth, European Women, and the Christological Crisis*. London: SPCK, 1995.

Hoyt, T. "Christology and the African-American Pilgrimage." In *Christology in Dialogue*, edited by R. F. Berkey and S. A. Edwards, 292–307. Cleveland: Pilgrim Press, 1993.

Khalidi, T., ed. *The Muslim Jesus: Saying and Stories in Islamic Literature*. Cambridge, MA: Harvard University Press, 2001.

Kirk, J. A. *Liberation Theology: An Evangelical View from the Third World*. Basingstoke: Marshall, Morgan & Scott, 1979, parts 3 and 4.

Knitter, P. F. *Jesus and Other Names: Christian Mission and Global Responsibility*. Maryknoll, NY: Orbis Books, 1996.

Küster, V. *The Many Faces of Jesus Christ: Intercultural Christology*. London: SCM Press, 2001.

Lilburne, G. "Christology: In Dialogue with Feminism." *Horizons* 11 (1984): 7–27.

Miranda, J. *Marx and the Bible: A Critique of the Philosophy of Oppression*. London: SCM Press, 1977, introduction and chap. 1.

Need, S. W. "Re-Reading the Prologue: Incarnation and Creation in John 1:1–18." *Theology* 106 (2003): 397–404.

Norman, E. *Christianity and the World Order*. Oxford: Oxford University Press, 1979, chap. 4.

Oduyoye, M. A. "Jesus Christ." In *The Cambridge Companion to Feminist Theology*, edited by S. F. Parsons, 151–70. Cambridge: Cambridge University Press, 2002.

Okure, T. "The Global Jesus." In *The Cambridge Companion to Jesus*, edited by M. Bockmuehl, 237–49. Cambridge: Cambridge University Press, 2001.

Panikkar, R. *Christophany: The Fullness of Man*. Maryknoll, NY: Orbis Books, 2004.

Parratt, J., ed. *An Introduction to Third World Christologies*. Cambridge: Cambridge University Press, 2004.

Pawlikowski, J. T., OSM. "Christology, Anti-Semitism, and Christian-Jewish Bonding." In *Reconstructing Christian Theology*, edited by R. S. Chopp and M. L. Taylor, 245–68. Minneapolis: Fortress Press, 1994.

Ratzinger, J. *Libertatis Nuntius*. London: Catholic Truth Society, 1984, 26–27.

Rigby, C. L. "Scandalous Presence: Incarnation and Trinity." In *Feminist and Womanist Essays in Reformed Dogmatics*, edited by A. P. Pauw and S. Jones, 58–74. Louisville, KY: Westminster John Knox Press, 2006.

Robinson, N. *Christ in Islam and Christianity*. Albany: State University of New York Press, 1991.

Ruether, R. R. *To Change the World: Christology and Cultural Criticism*. London: SCM Press, 1981.

Schreiter, R. J., ed. *Faces of Jesus in Africa*. Maryknoll, NY: Orbis Books, 1991.

Schüssler Fiorenza, E. *Jesus—Miriam's Child, Sophia's Prophet: Critical Issues in Feminist Christology*. New York: Continuum, 1994, 97–128.

Shuster, M., and R. Muller, eds. *Perspectives on Christology: Essays in Honour of Paul K. Jewett*. Grand Rapids: Zondervan, 1991.

Siddiqui, M. "The Image of Christ in Islam: Scripture and Sentiment." In *Images of Christ: Ancient and Modern*, edited by S. E. Porter, M. A. Hayes, and D. Tombs, 159–72. Sheffield: Sheffield Academic Press, 1997.

Snyder, M. *The Christology of Rosemary Radford Ruether: A Critical Introduction*. Mystic, CT: Twenty-Third Publications, 1988.

Sobrino, J. *Christology at the Crossroads*. London: SCM Press; Maryknoll, NY: Orbis Books, 1978.

———. *Jesus the Liberator: A Historical Theological Reading of Jesus of Nazareth*. Maryknoll, NY: Orbis Books, 1993.

Song, C. S. *Jesus, the Crucified People*. Minneapolis: Fortress Press, 1996.

Stevens, M., ed. *Reconstructing the Christ Symbol: Essays in Feminist Christology*. Mahwah, NJ: Paulist Press, 1993.

Sugirtharajah, R. S., ed. *Asian Faces of Jesus*. London: SCM Press, 1993.

Thistlethwaite, S. B., and M. P. Engel, eds. *Lift Every Voice: Constructing Christian Theologies from the Underside*. Rev. and exp. Maryknoll, NY: Orbis Books, 1998, 193–220.

Wessels, A. *Images of Jesus: How Jesus Is Perceived and Portrayed in Non-European Cultures.* Grand Rapids: Wm B. Eerdmans; London: SCM Press, 1990.

White, V. *Atonement and Incarnation: An Essay in Universalism and Particularity.* Cambridge: Cambridge University Press, 1991.

Witvliet, T. *The Way of the Black Messiah.* Oak Park, IL: Meyer-Stone Books; London: SCM Press, 1987.

Young, P. D. "Diversity in Feminist Christology." *Studies in Religion* 21 (1992): 81–90.

# Index of Subjects

125

# Index of Names

Abraham, 4, 10
Adam, 7, 8
Amaladoss, Michael, 102
Amoah, Elizabeth, 99
Ancoratus, 18
Anselm, 106
Apollinarius, x, 19, 21
Appasamy, A. J., 100
Aquinas, xi
Aristotle, 114
Arius, x, 17, 53–54
Athanasius, x, xi, 8, 19, 51, 53, 54, 114

Baker, John Austin, 58
Balthasar, Hans Urs von, xii, 61, 84
Banerjee, K. M., 100
Barth, Karl, 44, 65, 69
Battles, Ford Lewis, 55
Bauckham, R., 14, 15, 16
Benedict XVI, Pope, xi, 83
Bernard, 106
Boff, Leonardo, xii, 82
Brown, David, 113
Bultmann, Rudolf, x, 33–40, 45

Calvin, John, xi, 55
Campbell, J. Y., 36
Casey, M., 13–14
Cavadini, John C., 85
Chakkarai, V., 100

Chenchiah, P., 100
Chester, Andrew, 13
Cleage, Albert, 97
Coakley, Sarah, xii, 7, 24, 93
Cone, James H., 96, 97
Crossan, John Dominic, 39
Cunton, Colin E., 36
Cupitt, Don, x, 26, 60
Cyril of Alexandria, 21, 24, 54

Dante, 33
Davis, Stephen T., xi, 24, 62
Dionysius, 33

Elijah, 2, 3
Engel, Mary Potter, 96
Epiphanius, 18
Eskola, T., 15, 16
Eusebius of Caesarea, 115
Ezekiel, 15, 105, 106

Fabella, Virginia, 100
Farquhar, J. N., 101
Farrer, Austin, xi, 73, 74, 78
Feenstra, Robert .J., ix, 5
Fiorenza, Elisabeth Schüssler, 91
Forsyth, P. T., xi, 56

Galloway, Allan D., 45
Goethe, 33